POWER SPEAKING

By
Mark Yarnell

Editor: Jennifer L. Osborn

Cover Design: Knight Abbey Graphics & Printing, Biloxi MS
Cover Photo: Cliff Warner

PAPER CHASE PRESS New Orleans LA

POWER
SPEAKING

PAPER CHASE PRESS
5721 Magazine St., Suite 152
New Orleans LA 70115

Printed in the United States

ACKNOWLEDGMENTS

I owe a warm debt of thanks to my editor, Jennifer Osborn, whose skills have helped make this the best book on public speaking available today. I also wish to thank my family for their patience and support during the writing process.

Mark Yarnell

INTRODUCTION

Power Speaking is the key to your success.

Why?   Power Speaking is a means of communicating effectively and with impact.   Power Speaking is also a way of thinking. As a Power Speaker, you learn to communicate at a higher level than most because you learn to adopt a higher level of thinking. The benefits of learning Power Speaking can be quite remarkable.

Despite all the communications technology of today, few people put emphasis on the ability to speak. And the fact is, the more effective you are at communicating your ideas, your thoughts, and your feelings, the more likely you can achieve success.

Speaking effectively, indeed, speaking with impact and power, begins with careful and well reasoned thought. Speaking with power is also balancing logical thought with just the right amount of emotion.   So, to speak powerfully you must not only clearly and logically get your point across, but you must affect the thoughts and emotions of the listener.

Power Speaking makes it possible for anyone with the interest and the initiative to make a positive and dramatic change in their life, to learn how to think and speak powerfully. And once having learned these principles it will become very clear why Power Speaking is the key to your success.

Read, learn, and prepare for the remarkable changes in your life.

Jennifer L. Osborn
Editor

CONTENTS

"Whate'er is well conceived is clearly said,
And the words to say it flow with ease."

> ~Nicolas Boileau-Despréaux (1636-1711)
> *The Art of Poetry*

"A word fitly spoken is like apples of gold in pictures of silver."

> ~The Holy Bible, Proverbs 25:11

"Remember you are a human being with a soul and the divine gift of articulate speech: that your language is the language of Shakespeare and Milton and The Bible and don't sit there crooning like a bilious pigeon."

> ~George Bernard Shaw
> *"Pygmalion"*

Chapter 1

What Power Speaking Means

Human beings are able to communicate nearly everything and anything in the spoken word. When we feel happiness, anger, love, pain, enthusiasm, when we wish to persuade, encourage, or sell, when we want to alert, protect, defend, and negotiate, when we need to communicate our thoughts, our ideas, our inspirations, our knowledge, our goals, the spoken word is often the best and most effective way to communicate to another person or people. However, few people try to develop the ability to communicate clearly and effectively. Most people are content to talk without thinking a great deal about what they are saying or how they deliver the words they say. They take for granted the marvelous ability they possess: the ability to speak.

Christ, Socrates, Lincoln, Kennedy....

Christ, Socrates, Lincoln, Churchill, Kennedy, Susan B. Anthony, Martin Luther King, and Margaret Thatcher. Nearly anyone who knows some history has heard of any or all of these great people. What do they all have in common? They were all known for being very effective speakers. To a large extent, their success was based on their ability to move people by speaking, either individually or while addressing multitudes of people at one time.

In fact, Christ and Socrates were known only for what they said, because they never actually wrote anything. It took admirers and observers to record that these men were remarkable speakers, and to record what these men said. If you think about the effect these men had on the world all because of what they said, you can imagine how effective they were as speakers.

Effective speaking does not merely convey ideas, but inspires, motivates and instructs all at the same time. Effective speaking involves not only capturing the attention of listeners, but maintaining their interest. Leaders like Christ and Socrates instinctively knew this and spoke powerfully even though they were never given formal speech instruction.

Ford, Rockefeller, Disney...

There are many successful businessmen known to have succeeded largely because they were (or are) very effective speakers. In the past, there was Henry Ford, John D. Rockefeller, Andrew Carnegie, and Walt Disney, to name a handful. Walt Disney, for example, raised ten million dollars to start Disneyland, based almost entirely on painting a picture with words of the world's first theme oriented amusement park. Anyone else less able to convey his ideas with words would have come across as a madman. But Disney knew how to capture the imaginations of his financiers and inspire them to give him millions.

More recently, such men as Lee Iacocca, Donald Trump, and F. Lee Bailey have developed the reputation for being very effective speakers. Trump is so effective in speaking that he was able to persuade nearby New York bankers to finance the purchase and remodeling of an old hotel to become the beautiful Grand Hotel — a building worth hundreds of millions of dollars today — which he owns without having had to capitalize with any of his own money.

Speaking with Power

Words have power. The written word has power, hence the common expression: "The pen is mightier than the sword." But someone able to wield the spoken word powerfully can wield almost unimaginable power. Entire corporations employing hundreds and possibly thousands have been built because someone was able to speak powerfully; even whole nations and people have been moved because of the powerful words of one person.

Most people reading this book may aspire to succeed and achieve greatness to the extent that they can, but will most likely never be the founders of big companies or govern a country. Instead, you, the reader, are probably more concerned about perhaps building a small or medium sized company from scratch, trying to make a profit, or you're just trying to manage a group of employees at your place of work. Or you are a salesperson with the aim of increasing your sales territory, clientbase, or downline. Or maybe you are involved with a non-profit organization or some worthwhile cause seeking funding. Or perhaps you are just interested in learning to communicate more effectively with people close to you. In any case, you have chosen to read this book most likely because you have realized the need to communicate more effectively with people, in the work environment and elsewhere. You want results and you sense that speaking clearly and strongly is the key.

What I call Power Speaking is actually a proven method to speak to people either individually or in groups (of nearly any size) to achieve what the great speakers have been able to do for generations: to effectively inspire, motivate and inform their listeners. Like anything in life there is usually a right way and a wrong way. I have personally tried both the right and wrong ways to communicate to people. I have been trained in a seminary to teach and preach. I have studied the university courses on speech and public speaking, and I have been giving professional speeches for years.

Through my own knowledge and experience, and through the things I have learned from other excellent speakers, I have cultivated what I know to be the best way to construct and deliver a speech, or at least to talk to people and relate to them more effectively, one on one.

Power Speaking is not something you automatically come into this world knowing. Granted, there are people who apparently have the natural gift to speak clearly and effectively. But even they will have to admit to making a concerted effort at doing so, and will also admit to being prepared in advance to speak the way they do. Power Speaking is not done entirely by fate or accident. To speak and communicate powerfully requires adequate instruction and repeated application. Just as with playing a musical instrument, instruction and practice can hone and perfect one's speaking skills.

In the chapters which follow, you will get the basics about Power Speaking. You will learn to think and perform in the way necessary to succeed as an effective speaker. Anyone reading this material, no matter what your initial interest in speaking may have been, will benefit. However, I put particular emphasis on speaking before groups of people, whether for small informal meetings, for formal business meetings, or for professional lectures and talks. Emphasis is placed particularly on group speaking because it is the most common situation in which most people will find themselves.

One issue I deal with is the fear of speaking before groups of people. Fear is the most common yet unnecessary hindrance to most people when it comes to speaking. Once you learn how to *think* the right way and learn how to *deliver* a power speech, and you have made several speeches, the fear will dissipate. Stage fright can affect even the best of speakers, but once you go into action, the fright diminishes or simply goes away. Moreover, you will begin to realize that you are building your level of confidence not only to speak, but also to pursue other things in life.

The last part of this book provides details about becoming a professional speaker. This will not be everyone's interest, but learning about professional speaking can be useful perhaps later on, as a new career, or possibly to provide insight on how to deal with speakers should you be in a position to hire them for your group. Should you wish to become a professional speaker, I reveal the best way to present yourself to people for speaking engagements, and the best ways to look for and secure speaking engagements.

Immediate Benefits of Power Speaking

Although you may have long term goals of increasing your sales territory, or increasing profits, or getting funding, or whatever, as the result of becoming a Power Speaker, you will experience other tangible and immediate benefits from your ability to deliver a Power Speech. Any time someone makes a good, powerful speech several things generally happen:

+ you build self confidence
+ listeners get the impression that you are an authority
+ you create an aura of expertise
+ you generate for yourself a star quality

These days poise and credibility have a lot to do with success. Self confidence instills respect in the people around you. You can be assured that a well delivered speech is appreciated and people let you know this. The result is a tremendous boost in your self confidence.

What's interesting is that your poise, that is, your air of confidence, will give you credibility. Then you will discover that speaking effectively, whether in small or large groups, combined with confidence, has a way of immediately establishing you as an authority on whatever topic you are talking about. So, naturally, if you are an authority, you no doubt possess the expertise in the topic.

People always want to be near me and seek my attention after I make a speech. People in a position of power and influence want to be associated with me. Why? Because I have become the object of attention by just about anyone in attendance. I have become a "star," a sort of celebrity in their eyes.

Can the sort of attention you receive as a Power Speaker help you in business or at your job? No question about it. I know of many people who have attended my Power Speaking seminars and have related to me how their enhanced speaking skills and speeches have directly led to various business opportunities (i.e., new jobs, increased business, etc.).

For example, Gary Keller of Austin, Texas, applied his Power Speaking skills to make speeches at the various business groups in Austin including the Rotary Club and the Lions Club.   These engagements were instrumental in making the contacts he needed to build the sixth largest real estate business in the state of Texas with over 40 million dollars in sales the first year.

Another example is a former president of the American Society of Association Executives who attended a Power Speaking seminar (which I no longer do) and applied his speaking skills during business meetings and conferences he had to address. His abilities were noticed and before long he was hired to be president of one of America's largest savings and loans.

Then there is Deborah Hampton who, until she had attended one of my seminars, was shy and very uncomfortable speaking to groups of more than two or three people. However, once she began applying her Power Speaking skills, which she honed during speeches she gave at her local Toastmasters, she began receiving invitations to speak. Before long, she approached me to become a trained Power Speaking seminar instructor.   Six months later, Deborah was conducting Power Speaking seminars for Fortune 500 corporate executives in her home town, Park City, Utah. Deborah has been a Power Speaking seminar instructor for several years now.

One thing I noticed is that if you develop strong speaking skills, this is something people come to respect. And if you indicate an interest in speaking, you will be invited to more and more speaking engagements.   Before long, you will either make money as a professional speaker (because there is always a demand for good speakers and the money is excellent), land a new job (because someone listened to your speech and was impressed by how you handled yourself; this is quite common), be promoted in the company where you work (because your speaking has elevated your visibility in the company), or be offered any number of business opportunities (because often, people want to be associated with someone who is a good speaker, particularly if you are a professional speaker: the "star" quality effect). The secret is: the more you do, the more you will be able to do in the long run.

Power Speaking Audio Tape

The book you are now reading contains all you need to know in order to enhance your speaking skills and succeed as a powerful, effective speaker. However, should you wish step-by-step instruction and to have an audio recorded example of an actual speech I've made hundreds of times, and which has made me nearly a million dollars, you should purchase my *Power Speaking* audio tape (details on ordering the tape at the end of this book). And even without the tape, my book, *Power Speaking*, should be your continual source of direction and encouragement as you develop your speaking skills.

Chapter 2

The Power Speech

In Power Speaking, simplicity controls everything, from how to make moves for personal attainment to how to learn and use Power Speaking principles. Simplicity is the best example of good teaching. I am going to get you up in front of a group of people as fast as possible, fearlessly, with a high level of polish.

You will find that polish requires remarkably little effort once you have some simple instruction. Polish will overcome fear, not practice alone. Remember: if you practice a bad speech a thousand times, it will still be bad.

> *The focus of Power Speaking is construction.*

Once you know how to construct a powerful presentation and have a few basics on how to deliver it, you will have turned the act of speaking in front of groups from failure to success.

A common misconception is that there is a different style and type of presentation to prepare and deliver for each of the many possible public speaking settings. For a convention, there is one type of presentation; for a sales meeting another; and for a civic association, yet another. In one setting, you are supposed to entertain. In another, you are supposed to teach and inform, and so on.

This notion is one of the most confusing and erroneous concepts regarding public speaking. It tends to enshroud public or group speaking in mystique by creating the impression that incredible knowledge and talent are necessary to successfully accomplish it. That is not true. Attempting to adapt a different style and format to all possible engagements is a waste of your valuable time and energy.

> **Simplicity is your best approach in public speaking.**

There is only one type of presentation for all settings: all Power Speeches must entertain, inspire, and teach. Though there are all sorts of reasons for a person to speak before groups, to reap the most from the opportunities, *all presentations must motivate and teach.* You want the audience to remember and recognize you. To accomplish that, you must bring to listeners something important to them personally, inspire and motivate them to take action, and then teach them a way to take the action to improve their lives.

What about an award ceremony, or a weekly sales meeting, or a women's club chapter meeting? The motivational aspect doesn't have to be of monumental proportions or universal implications. It could be about increasing sales, how to grow a better flower, or as important as living life without stress or getting love back into your life. If you stop and think this through, you will find there is not a single case where motivation and inspiration of some sort can not be used as the underlying purpose of any talk or presentation.

But motivation and inspiration alone are not enough. You doubtless have seen many presentations where the speaker identified a problem, built the audience to a fever pitch by motivating it to action, and then failed to tell them what kind of action to take or how to take it.

> ***How-to's are an essential part of the Power Speech.***

What happens if you leave out appropriate methods — "how-to's" — to accomplish suggestions you make? Listeners are motivated or inspired temporarily but don't remember the talk for more than a few hours. They don't change their lives for the better and ultimately you have wasted their time.

What is a "how-to"? It is not a convoluted plan of action that takes a speaker hours to explain. Instead, it might be a little phrase. For example, imagine you are presenting a talk to a group of salespeople on the importance of "closing" on every client call; that is, asking the client to buy something every time a salesperson makes a contact. One of your points in the talk is that closings provoke anxiety because of the fear of rejection. Because of that fear, many salespeople avoid closings whenever possible. But closing every time is what makes people top producers. So the more closings, the better the production. You must have a way to overcome the fear of closing. Therefore, at the end of this particular point in the presentation, you suggest, "Before you make any call to a client, sit and think, 'this client has to buy my product or service to do his work and stay in business. He needs me and my product.' You must convince yourself first." This is a how-to.

Another example could be this: suppose you are giving a presentation about how to fight the blues. Your how-to could suggest people use a "joy calendar" to record joyous days of past years to help them focus on those things that bring happiness. In both cases, the how-to is a simple instruction, not a complicated plan.

One how-to is used for each point in the speech. One point, one how-to. If not, the presentation is overloaded, off balance, and the audience is confused about the topic. Laundry lists of suggested changes people can make are boring and confusing.

With the proper how-to's, listeners have something to take home (i.e., a way to solve a problem or fulfill a promise on which they have been motivated to act). They *will* remember the speech and the speaker.

> *You cannot accomplish anything of substance through public speaking without providing how-to's.*

As there is only one type of speech, there is only one format to use. The format is the key to drafting any speech. You need only one format. When you become more proficient and adept, you'll find that you can pare it down a little into a sort of sub-format. By then, though, you will have seen the power of the format and will understand, through practical application, the underlying elements of the format and how to maintain its integrity.

It is this format that will keep you from going overboard on the how-to's or humor and will allow you to use all the elements needed to accomplish the goal of entertaining, motivating, and teaching.

Balance is the goal of a well-prepared and well-delivered Power Speech and is achieved with the proper format. A smooth, coherent relationship among the elements of the presentation will prevent you from falling into a lot of traps that may have kept you from succeeding in the past. Balance will keep you from straying from the path of a power presentation by assuring that no one of the elements of the speech overshadows the others, that no elements are omitted, and that the topic is never abandoned.

> *Balance is what keeps your listeners in tune with your message.*

What does it mean to have balance in your speech? The importance of how-to's and how to use them is one example.   Another is examining the use of humor.

The proper use of humor in a Power Speech is essential. Improper use of humor probably destroys more talks and speakers than any other element of public speaking. In almost every speech I have witnessed, humor was out of balance with the rest of the speech and reduced the message to a minor consideration.

One reason humor often overbalances the rest of the speech is the speaker's overconcern with its use. Most people are as afraid of telling a joke in front of a crowd as they are afraid of giving speeches in general. The thought of having to tell a joke to a group of three to fifty people is enough to stop many from speaking altogether.

However, a more prevalent reason humor overrides a presentation is the result of a notion that the primary purpose of a presentation is to entertain, and the only way to entertain a crowd is with an endless string of jokes. You've seen this countless times. Even if the setting was instructional, the speaker told joke after joke because he believed if he could make his audience laugh, he could impress them. And he might have for a few minutes, but that is all, because the message was lost, motivation was ignored, and instruction was thrown away.

I have solved this potential problem two ways. One, as it has already been proven, all speeches must be entertaining, motivational, *and* instructional.   Second, I have prepared a format to use in all settings to achieve a proper balance to assure all three purposes can be accomplished. A speaker can't focus solely on entertaining and be able to motivate and instruct. You cannot be a jokester and a Power Speaker at the same time.   On the other hand, a motivator and instructor *can* be entertaining. A Power Speaker will get a standing ovation and audiences will leave with a new-found ability to change their lives for the better. The Power Speaker will be remembered.

I don't want to minimize humor. I just want you to know that your ability to succeed as a public speaker does not hinge on being funny. *It depends on balance and purpose.* There is a time, place, and reason for humor. The perfect time is determined and kept in balance by the format, as is the case with all the other elements of a presentation.

There are four main building blocks in the Power Speaking structure. Each speech, of course, has an introduction, a body, and a conclusion. In Power Speaking, a speech has:

- a powerful, thought-provoking introduction;
- a statement of your obligation to listeners;
- a body of well-thought out points; and
- a conclusion that inspires.

You make your points in the body of the speech with illustrations, inspirational stories or statements, humor, and how-to's. If any one of these elements overshadows the others, then the power of the speech is reduced.

The result of this cohesion and balance is a wonderful polish that exudes professionalism. Another reason to strive for harmony among the parts of a presentation is that you're usually under severe time constraints when speaking. Unless you have engineered a balance that assures that you cover all the points and meet all the objectives, you will run out of time to accomplish what you want.

Never speak more than twenty-five minutes. After twenty-five minutes of speaking, you begin to lose 80 to 85 percent of the listeners. After that, no matter how good the presentation, you begin to sound like one long monotonous drone. How many times have you drifted off because the speaker went on too long? Besides that, most chairs where meetings are held are not comfortable, and if you want to be uncomfortably distracted yourself, just wait until you see four hundred people wiggling in their chairs.

Actually, I like to speak twenty minutes. I find listeners appreciate it and are usually left wanting more. In small group settings or informal discussions, five or ten minutes is enough.

However, some groups ask for speakers to take an hour, or if it's a long business meeting or highly specialized informational event, even longer. Here's an easy way to handle that. Just tell the event chairman or manager of your company that you will only speak for twenty-five minutes. That's it. Tell him that you will open the floor for questions or discussion after that. If the setting calls for even more time, you can call for a coffee break every twenty-five minutes.

A more common occurrence, however, is that you will have much less than twenty-five minutes to speak. I'm thinking of less formal company discussions, opportunities at sales meetings, etc. Under those circumstances, your purpose in speaking is just as critical and, in fact, your ability to get your message across professionally may be even more important to you than formal presentations. Your temptation will be to speak off the cuff. Never do that!

When speaking to any group, you must always be prepared and rehearsed. It's easy to understand why preparation is necessary to deliver a speech to a convention or Lions Club meeting. Often, however, participants in Power Speaking seminars have tried to deny the importance of always being prepared. They have two claims:

1. Often it is impractical to prepare ahead of time, especially in small groups or informal settings; and
2. They believe they are actually very good at impromptu speaking.

To say one doesn't need to be prepared for a small group implies that the people in the group are not important because of the group's size. With that attitude, you automatically negate the importance of your message. What were you talking for, anyway? When you don't prepare, you steal away minutes of valuable time from the listeners.

Addressing preparation for informal settings is a stickier issue. In many situations, there is no apparent arena for which to prepare. But think about this for a moment. You go to a meeting where you know there is going to be a crossfire of comments. Ahead of time, you know what the meeting is going to be about. You may even have an agenda. You probably have an idea what other people's positions are before you go in. You also know, or should know, what you want to accomplish, what your position is, and that you need to state it. You know that there will be a turning point in the discussion at which you will want to make your position clear. But, you may have only five minutes to speak. Preparation is never more important than now. Clearly, you can prepare for such a situation. Clearly, you *must* prepare for it. *You will run into this scenario more than any other.*

Structure of a five-minute Power Speech

Make only one point in a five-minute speech. Support the point with the four elements: quotes or true stories, humor, inspiration, and a how-to. You must make a contract with the listeners, and end with some form of inspiration. As in all circumstances, preparation is important. You can prepare for these short speaking opportunities because you usually have an idea in advance of what you want to say and how the opportunity will arise.

The most likely example where preparation doesn't seem possible is spur-of-the-moment team or company meetings where you must make decisions on new products or directions for the company. Companies do this increasingly these days as an offshoot of employee input, and these meetings can be good opportunities for you. So, how do you prepare? It isn't as if you knew the subject and tenor of the meeting a day in advance.

Wait, listen, and prepare. Can you recall the admiration people have expressed over those who sit and listen quietly in meetings for long periods and then, just at the right moment, make the most pertinent statements? Everyone marvels at how the suggestion or information comes from nowhere and yet displays deep insight. Become that person. Take in what is being said and the drift of the meeting. Think of the point and develop it as others are talking. You have a format now; use it to develop the point. It works every time, and people walk away impressed by your contribution.

It seems simple, I know, but the point is, there are almost no circumstances in which Power Speaking will not work. The key is to be adept at using the principles and seeing the possibilities. Do not stay locked into your previous limitations. You must use your head and be flexible. Another example of how you can be creative with the principles, especially in shorter talks, deals with inspiration.

Don't be afraid to use negative inspiration. Generally, you want to use positive inspiration to point out the good in people's lives and the high potential people can reach. However, it is sometimes difficult in a short talk at a long meeting to achieve an uplifting, positive tone. Or it may just be impossible to use positive inspiration when emphasizing a point.

Negative inspiration is a specific story or supposition of what would happen if the group didn't take action, or if they continued to follow a perilous path. For example, in a meeting about impending legislation that could doom a company's business, where you want to implore the group to work hard for the legislation's defeat, a horror story of what has happened to other businesses in similar circumstances can inspire the group to action. This is negative inspiration.

What about impromptu speaking?

No one is good at speaking off the cuff. It is unfair to listeners, and it makes it impossible to get your very important message across in a clear, balanced, and professional way, especially in a severely limited time frame. Why would you want to throw opportunities away?

You'll find as you become more proficient at these methods that your presentations will be so smooth they will seem off the cuff, and your preparation and assimilation time will diminish to the point at which it will seem almost impromptu to you, too.

Practice, practice, practice

With preparation goes practice. *After you have learned to construct a perfectly balanced, powerful speech, it's time to practice.* Practice alone is not the way to overcome fear or become a proficient speaker. However, after you have a professional vehicle, practice is essential in your drive for polish.

Never give a speech or presentation that you haven't practiced at least five times in front of a mirror with a cassette recorder or in front of a video recorder. Preferably, do it more. One major reason is that you have the opportunity to pare down the vehicle for the speech, your outline, to workable proportions and to realize what you can accomplish in the allotted time.

Power Speaking throws the manuscripts away forever. Preparation and practice allow you to speak with ease from a skeleton outline rather than from a manuscript. There is nothing duller than a speech read from a manuscript. You might as well just hand out copies and let everyone read it at their leisure. There really is nothing more to it than that.

Never overburden audiences with a glut of information. Practice and preparation, focusing on balance, help you overcome the tendency to overburden speeches with everything you know on the subject. It is difficult not to do this. But if you make up your mind that you are not going to load your listeners down with too much information, and convince yourself you do not need to create a world for your audience, your task will be easier.

There are two types of people in the audiences, those who don't know as much about the subject as you do, and those who know as much or more. Those who don't know as much as you will become confused by extensive detail and inside or intricate information that they don't need to know. Those who are at, or ahead of, your level already know the details and want to hear *your* impressions, conclusions, and instructions.

You want to aim for the macro-points of the subject, the big picture. Never provide a laundry list of, say, ten points. When you do that people start counting the points to make sure you get them all in and ignore the message. *Avoid the pitfalls of overinformation by showing that you need to make and support only three points.* Those three points can be as broad as the Grand Canyon, but they can be brought home to the audience in the most meaningful and concise ways, leaving audience members room to think and ponder. That is what you want. You cannot do all their thinking for them!

Never use visual aids. I call the use of visual aids the "Wizard of Oz" syndrome. People generally use visual aids to hide nervousness or to overshadow a poor presentation and lack of preparation. I know this ban against visual aids runs contrary to the way most people think a presentation should be made, especially in a corporate setting, where some companies almost require the use of visual aids. It's also contrary to what has been pounded into your head in speech classes and other instructional settings. Resist the temptation to use visuals and resist policy requirements to use them. There is never a need for visual aids, except perhaps in an all-day seminar setting or in a television address by the U.S. president or a newscaster.

In live and in-person presentations, visuals can be disastrous. How many times have you been in a business meeting and the speaker says, "Profits have risen five percent. As you can see on the screen, the graph shows profits have risen five percent"? What a boring waste of time! Visual aids are more than boring, they are distracting. Listeners often end up reading slides instead of listening to the speaker. If a group is reading slides instead of listening to you, then you are negating all your benefits as a speaker.

I meet a lot of resistance on accepting this point. Many seminar participants try to figure out reasons to break the rule — for example, at a sales meeting where a new car is being described. On such occasions, or if for any reason you believe you need some visual

representation of a point or fact, make copies and hand them out to
listeners. Do not distract the audience from what you are saying.

Chapter Review

Objective: Maximum efficiency with minimum effort using Power
Speaking

Focus: Speech construction without gimmicks

Purpose: One-type speech — entertaining, motivating, and
instructional

Vehicle: One format

Result: Always prepared, balanced presentation

Time: Never more than twenty-five minutes

Pitfalls: Overinformation, visual aids, manuscripts

Chapter 3

Opening:
The First Two Minutes

Imagine this kind of opening to a speech:

"Good evening, ladies and germs. Ha, ha. [*Pause*] First of all, I would like to thank Bob very much for that wonderful introduction. . . and the great setup, too! Bob, [*glance to Bob*]. . . just what is a highly respected Spublic Peaker, anyway? [*Chuckle*] Now we know why those of you in the audience who work for Bob have a hard time getting your work done. . . Bob's instructions. Right? [*Pause*] I would like to thank [*glancing down the head table*] Mr. Smith, Mrs. Robinson, Mr. Dundee, and most of all, you, Mr. Bledsoe, for having me here tonight. [*To audience*] And I want to thank all of you [*cough, clearing of throat*]. . . Excuse me. . . . Sorry. I want to thank all of you very much for coming and listening. It's a real pleasure to be here. I am here tonight to talk about something of very grave importance to each and every one of us in this room, but before I do, I want to relate something. A funny thing happened on the way to the meeting tonight. . . ."

By this time, we have long since tuned out the speaker, and he would be better off if he quit now. He does not do a single thing right. In fact, his introduction breaks every rule in this book about how to open a speech.

Make a good first impression. Most people embark on a speaking assignment by profusely thanking listeners and everyone else in the universe. In the world of Power Speaking, this is never done. At best, it is dull, and it often embarrasses both you and your listeners. For example, consider the manager who, upon taking over a division of one of the world's largest computer companies, opened his address to his new employees by saying, "Someone once told me to always thank the audience at the beginning of a speech, even if you don't think you have anything to thank them for. After all, there is always something you should be thankful for. So, thank you very much, it is a pleasure to be here." Well, it may have been a pleasure for him, but his listeners were not quite sure if the speaker had meant to insult them or if he was just extremely nervous.

Misconceptions and fallacies about public speaking abound, and most center on how to open a speech or talk. Here is a list of *nevers* for the opening of any presentation.

- Never thank the person who introduces you.
- Never thank people at the head table.
- Never thank the audience.
- Never excuse yourself for coughing, sneezing, or any reason.
- Never say, "It's a pleasure to be here."
- Never create an impromptu joke.
- Never be cute, glib, or coy with the audience.
- Never draw attention to mistakes made by your introducer.

> *In no other area of life is a good first impression as critical as it is in public speaking.*

Now you begin to learn how to construct a powerful, professional-quality speech. This is the format. The format is provided in two ways: by element and time. The first part of the speech is its *opening* and can last *no more than two minutes*.

Remember, you only have, at most, twenty-five minutes to get the message across. Because of time constraints, every minute of the presentation, whether a formal speech or a talk in a less formal setting, must be precisely calculated to meet a specific need for each audience, beginning with the opening two minutes and ending with the final words of inspiration.

In Power Speaking, no portion of a talk or presentation is insignificant. Yet, most speakers render the opening insignificant with parenthetical fluff such as thank yous, acknowledgments, off-the-cuff references to mistakes either by the speaker or other meeting participants, or impromptu humor. In so doing, *the vast majority of would-be quality speakers lose listeners in the first thirty seconds of the presentation.*

On the other hand, the speaker who has a provocative, polished, and powerful opening can hold his listeners even if the remainder of the presentation is mediocre.

The opening two minutes are critical to the success of every presentation. What you want to accomplish with the opening is to stimulate listeners, to elicit a reaction, to make them understand that they are going to hear something very important to them *personally.*

While you have them thinking, don't telegraph the message or points to be covered in the talk. After all, listeners have to have a reason to stay with you. All you want to impress listeners with is the idea that they have a purpose for being there, and that purpose is to make some improvement in their lives, no matter what the scale.

Humor can be a disadvantage. Here's why you negate any possibility of a thought-provoking first impression with a "thank you" or impromptu humor.

The audience's first reaction is to your first words. "Thank you" elicits *no* reaction. That is exactly the opposite result you want.

Impromptu humor is even riskier. It could be bad, it is always irrelevant, it is a waste of time, and it is often alienating.

A smart off-the-cuff remark finding fault with an introducer or an attempt to be cute or flippant does nothing to set the stage for what the audience is about to hear and which the introduction is supposed to make them want to hear.

The temptation to be witty is great. Usually, MCs at meetings offer many opportunities for friendly barbs.   Many otherwise responsible people who often become program chairmen and are assigned the task of making introductions, are equipped with only a bio card to read from when introducing a speaker. And most of these well-meaning program chairmen have never learned to read in front of an audience, especially from a podium into a microphone. In nine out of ten cases, program chairmen will make three to five errors. Most people find the urge to make witty remarks at this point almost irresistible.   But don't interpret someone else's mistake as a great opportunity for a Power Speaker to create interest. Speakers who go ahead and fall prey to the temptation do so only to satisfy their own egos and not the needs of listeners. If you fall prey to the temptation, you will minimize your message by making your first comments relate to nothing important.

> *Do any of these things — acknowledgments, impromptu humor, thank you's — and you give the first impression of a bumbling, inconsequential presentation.*

I know this not only from observation but from hard knocks, too.   Before learning Power Speaking, I made every one of the above-mentioned errors at a national convention several years ago. I had been asked to speak to a group of five hundred people on an issue that affects the listeners intensely — their current income, even the possibility of losing their livelihoods. Before the evening of speeches, the group's executive committee had a dinner, and, as usual, wanted the keynote speaker there.

This group was particularly conservative. In fact, they were so conservative and well known for their stolidity that when the entertainment for the dinner started, I was taken aback. It was belly dancing. Nothing wrong with belly dancing; it just didn't seem to go with this group. Even more unusual, one of the gyrating, undulating females was a little nine year old girl. At the time and place, it all seemed rather unusual, actually bizarre.

I found out that most of the organization never knew what went on at the executive dinners. And not being schooled properly in how to open a speech, I, at the last minute, had been looking around for a good opening joke and thought this was a perfect opportunity. So, as an opening for the speech to the membership-at-large later in the evening, I joked about the belly dancers at the early dinner meeting. Can't remember the joke exactly. Would prefer not to.

Here's what happened. The executive committee did not want the membership to know what kind of entertainment they had enjoyed. They were mad because I told their little secret. The executives knew their constituency, who the executives believed would think the entertainment was in poor taste. The executives were right. The membership was upset because, indeed, they didn't believe belly dancing was tasteful, especially when I mentioned the nine year old girl. The members were hostile because I brought the message to them. You know the rest — about cutting the messenger's head off?

It was horrible. Even with the impact of the rest of the speech, it took almost twenty minutes to get the audience back. And then, it never really came around completely. The sad thing was, the information I had to share with them was of paramount importance to them. It was a ready-made issue. So not only did I reduce the value of the speech by opening with irrelevant thoughts, I alienated everyone in the room.

Remember, you want the opening of your presentation to create a positive response from listeners. They must be compelled to listen. *You must be polished, professional, and relevant at all times.* Here's how:

The structure of opening a Power Speech

For formal speeches and business gatherings, begin with what may seem like a very uncomfortable *pause of fifteen to twenty seconds*. During this pause, you are taking control of yourself and the audience. Do not be afraid of the silence (for less formal gatherings where you only have five to ten minutes, make the pause about five to ten seconds). During the pause, do *not* arrange notes, take off your watch, or fiddle with anything. During the pause, look out at the audience intently; pan the audience slowly. Then begin.

The proper opening consists of *only one* of three types of statements:

1. A thought-provoking statement or rhetorical question
2. An extremely humorous two minute anecdote
3. A very powerful illustration

Of the three, I believe the *first choice is best*:   a thought-provoking statement or rhetorical question. *I suggest that you avoid the other two choices.* The reason?

> *In the case of humor, most speakers are not expert enough to pull off a two minute humorous anecdote.*

More important, you risk giving the audience the impression that you are about to deliver a humorous presentation. The audience thinks this will be just one joke after another. But that's not what you intend at all, and your listeners have been deceived.

In the case of a powerful illustration, again, you must be very adept to do it well. Few people are capable of sustaining, or even finding, the degree of warmth or interpersonal charm necessary to pull it off. Also, it just isn't appropriate for many situations.

Don't worry. When you become a proficient Power Speaker, you'll know when and how to use either anecdotes or illustrations, if you get the urge. If you speak frequently, you may want to use them just for variety. But remember, they are never the preferred choice.

A powerful opening statement or rhetorical question has a great impact. Of course, everyone is capable of creating and delivering a powerful thought-provoking statement or rhetorical question. And no matter how broad the question, as long as it gets the audience thinking about change and makes them listen and respond, it is appropriate.

Here is an example of such a question and how it would be stated live to an audience. I use this opening, or a variation of it, over and over again, and it has never failed to do its job:

"If you had only a two to five month guarantee on life, how many of you would make changes today? Now before raising your hands, let me explain what I mean by this question. If you went to a doctor and found out you had terminal cancer, and then you went to another doctor for a second opinion, and he confirmed the diagnosis that you had terminal cancer and added that you had only five months to live — how many of you would change something in your life? Maybe the way you treat your spouse or friends. Maybe you would travel more. In fact, maybe you would cash in some of your life insurance or take out a loan to travel. Maybe you would quit your job. Now, if you had only a five month guarantee and would make some changes in your life, would you please raise your hands. . . ? Fine, I see that 99 percent of you would make changes. Now for the big question: those of you who *do* have a five month guarantee from tonight, would you raise your hands?"

Envision, now, this opening. Think of the pregnant pause; listen to yourself ask the question. Can you see the difference, feel its effectiveness and power over undirected thank-yous and uncalculated wit?

This type of question can be used in many settings. It forces people to really think about where they are in life without revealing the content of the speech. It forces listeners to reevaluate priorities. It creates excitement in the audience about what is going to be said from that point on. In fact, it suggests that what you are about to do is share ideas that are positive and enlightening, ideas that will enable the listeners to make changes they may have been thinking about for a long time. Some people actually feel you are giving them justification to make changes they have been wanting to make.

My five-months-to-live question always elicits response. I have been approached by numerous corporate executives who have thanked me and said that the question itself — the opening two minutes — was worth the price of admission for the whole talk.

A positive aspect of this kind of broad, provocative opening is that it doesn't bind you in any way. You can delve into almost any topic, so long as the topic prescribes some kind of change. And any message you bring is supposed to require some kind of change or improvement. Your opening question points out the need for change and sets the audience up so that they're ready to listen.

Of course, my specific opening question, or a similar provocative question you might design, lends itself best to an after-dinner speech, but it can be used in a corporate setting. However, sometimes you will want something a little different, especially in a corporate setting, i.e., a sales meeting or a board meeting.

Creating your opening statement

How you come up with an opening question or statement is simple. Consider the specifics of your presentation and then reconstruct the individual points to fit the larger idea of the overall problem or message and how it relates to the big picture of personal lives. It is micro-to-macro-thinking. It is the reverse of the way most people are taught to approach problems: we are usually instructed to approach a problem by breaking it down into its minute parts. Instead, my approach to creating an opening is to take the minute parts and put them back together until you have reached a universal subject (at least to listeners). Life is universal. Joy is universal. Dollars are universal to salesmen as is the beauty of flowers to a garden club.

Say, for example, flagging enthusiasm in your company has led to poor or reduced sales. Your talk will present three ways to improve attitudes to increase sales. Now think about your salespeople. What do they want? Don't they want to increase their incomes, or at least shouldn't they want to? So you could construct a statement like this:

"How many of you are honestly earning more money than you need? Would you please raise your hands? (*pause*) I mean really enough. . . to send your kids to any college where they will be accepted. . . to go on any trip. . . to buy your spouse something extravagant, not because he or she demands it, but just because you want to do it? Can you pay your debts? Will you have enough to retire? Can you kick back from work for a few weeks and not wonder where the next buck is going to come from? What if you got cancer? Now, who in here can say they have enough money? (*pause*) Now for a more important question. Wouldn't you have almost enough — not to burn, but for a lot of those things you want and need — if your sales increased dramatically? Couldn't you sell a lot more with tremendous vigor and enthusiasm?"

You could direct a similar question a number of ways, expand or contract on it, depending on the time allotted. The point is, a speaker must prime the audience to respond to him on the most personal level to receive the essence of the presentation with the most positive results.

A note on practice

I mentioned that practice was not the means to overcome fear or improve a bad speech. Only professional construction and delivery can do that. Once you have learned how to construct and deliver a speech, then practice is valuable. I also mentioned that you should practice each presentation *at least* five times. Here's an exception: *practice the opening two minutes at least a dozen times. Preferably more.*

The opening to your speech must be rock solid. You must be confident, poised, and polished. It will set the entire tone for your speech. A good opening can ensure success even if the rest of the speech is mediocre.

> *A rule of thumb: A bad beginning will ruin the best speech.*

Chapter Review

- ◆ The first two minutes of the speech are critical and cannot be treated lightly. Bomb the opening and lose listeners, no matter how important the message.

- ◆ The beginning of a presentation is never more than two minutes.

- ◆ Contrary to popular belief and practice, never thank anyone in a speech.

- ◆ There is never any occasion to respond to the person making introductions.

- ◆ Never ad-lib or attempt off-the-cuff humor.

- ◆ The introduction is always completely planned and calculated. Rehearse it a dozen or more times.

- ◆ Before beginning, pause for 15 to 20 seconds, intently panning the audience.

- ◆ Do not shuffle notes, take watch off, fiddle with anything at all.

- ◆ The most successful way to open a speech is with a provocative statement or rhetorical question. It is the easiest to construct and the most likely to evoke the desired listener response.

Chapter 4

The Contract:
The Next Thirty Seconds

Several years ago, the Austin Speakers' Bureau, an organization that provides professional speakers for meetings, mailed out a questionnaire to many of the nation's leading speakers.

This was the fifth question: *which thirty-second period of any talk or speech is the most important?* One hundred and fifty speakers responded. Without exception, they all answered the question *incorrectly*.

The reason? They didn't know about the speaker's contract. Even the most successful speakers are unaware of a specific time slot and a specific task that must take place in that time slot for a presentation to be of the highest quality.

The most important thirty seconds in any speech is the *speaker's contract* with listeners. It always immediately follows the two-minute opening. Of course, some successful speakers occasionally provide a contract, but always by accident. When they do, it is never calculated or planned, as everything in public speaking should be. The contract is often mistimed and misplaced. But most often, the speaker's contract is missing.

Over a decade ago, I developed the concept of what to do with the next thirty seconds—the idea of a speaker's contractual obligation with listeners — in an effort to create the *ultimate Power Speech*. What exactly is the contract?

> **The contract tells listeners what you, the speaker, will do for them if they will listen to you.**

I cannot overemphasize how valuable a contract will be to you as a Power Speaker. Your use of a contract will ensure your success and immediately establish you as a professional-quality speaker. The contract is innovative and creative, and it will enable you to reach tremendous heights of public speaking prowess.

Before I provide the specifics of construction and delivery of contracts, you need to understand why these bold contentions are true and why I created the concept of making a contract with an audience.

Why use a contract? To be the best speaker possible, a speaker must always be mindful of the listeners' position. It is the only way to communicate powerfully. So understand that the listeners have given you, the speaker, a precious commodity: their time. They have given you the next twenty-five minutes (or less, in some cases), which they can never retrieve. Therefore, by being there, they have fulfilled one element of a contract with you and that is their willingness to take time to listen. They are the ones who have formed a contract with you. What is your part of the bargain? What are you going to do for the listeners? Are they justified in spending their time?

In this thirty seconds after the opening, tell listeners what you will do for them to let them know they have made a wise decision by listening to you.

Another reason I created the contract was to counter and replace one of the *worst* pieces of advice ever perpetrated on speakers: "tell them what you are going to tell them, tell them, and then tell them what you told them." Even though this approach is weak and wrong, almost every speaker uses it to direct the construction of his speeches and presentations.

Do not believe that this ploy is what I am getting at when I speak of the contract. It is the exact opposite.

Telling listeners, in advance, specifics of what you are going to say, even in encapsulated form, robs them of a reason to listen. It negates the message and runs contrary to my philosophy that you must give listeners a reason to consciously stay for the duration of the presentation. No amount of digression or expansion on those telegraphed points will counter the fact that you have already told the audience what you want to say, so they might as well go home or into some far-off daydream. Reiterating information at the end only amounts to so much redundancy — just more wasted time.

On the other hand, the contract I speak of is not an encapsulation of the speech. It is only a statement that directly and boldly gives the audience a reason for being there. Its purpose is to stimulate and excite listeners so that they believe they must listen to what you have to say. The contract tells the audience that, in your opinion, what you have to say will have a dramatic impact on them.

Use these three ingredients to construct and deliver a successful basic contract with the audience:

1. Exaggerate within reason. One purpose of a contract is to excite listeners. They must believe they should be there listening. You must appeal to the highest aspirations both of the individual and of the total group. That is what will push the individual listener's button.

Let me explain. Here is an example of a contract: "If you do what I am about to suggest, you could close 50 percent more of your clients beginning today."

Of course, this is hyperbole. Not every salesman, if he listens, will close 50 percent more new accounts or his existing clientele fifty percent of the time. But the best of the salesmen might. Salesmen know that. They want to believe that they could be the best salesman. You offer the highest expectations for fulfillment. This is exaggeration within reason. I didn't say 100 or 110 percent of clients could be closed. That would be ridiculous and listeners would know it; therefore, you would have no credibility.

On the other hand, if you don't gear the contractual statement to the best in the group — suppose you said, ". . . closings might increase ten to fifteen percent, on average. . . ," you've suggested mediocrity or limitations. What appeal does that have?

Reasonable hyperbole appeals to another type of listener, too, a person I call the *willing skeptic*. You'll find that sometimes a minority of your listeners will be skeptical at this point. Often, they are the more intelligent listeners. The willing skeptic is the one who leans back and says to himself, "Oh, yeah? Show me." That doesn't matter to you because you are going to show him. In any event, that person will listen closely. That's what you want.

2. Be sincere. The contract is a time to be serious. It is no time to be flippant. It would help greatly if you have picked a subject in which you believe strongly and have developed points you truly believe will fulfill the promises you make.

3. Be excited almost to the point of overexuberance. This calls on you to use a bit of theatrics. I am not talking about complex movements or inflections or anything like that. It comes from your frame of mind.

You must stress, strongly and openly, with your voice, eyes, and mannerisms, that what you are saying is important to you and your listeners. You should take some time to sell yourself on the idea that what you are giving to your listeners is *truly* important. If you don't believe it is with all your heart, then you have no business being there.

Once you have convinced yourself that you are going to give listeners some winning information, then think back to the last time you related to someone close to you a story of a very dramatic incident in your life. It could have been about the birth of your first child, when you hit the winning home run or scored a touchdown, closed the biggest business deal of your life, when you were almost run off the road by an eighteen-wheeler, or when you pulled off a delicate political maneuver in the office. You might imagine how exciting it would be to win a million dollars in the lottery. Anything exciting at all, just remember what it felt like.

Do you remember how you emphasized key words? How your voice raised and lowered? How you held your hands when you wanted your friend to understand what had happened?

If you relate the contract the same way you related an exciting story to a friend, you'll be okay. The key is to believe that what you are about to say will be beneficial to listeners. The reason for all this excitement is that you have to excite listeners, and the best way for you to do it is to be excited and exuberant. It spills over, and the audience is primed.

How do you gauge if you have properly constructed and delivered the contract? Frequently, after the best opening and contract, listeners will pull out paper and pen because they realize what they are about to hear is critical to them. If when you make your contract, at least a few people don't begin to record your message in writing, then you must question the effectiveness of the contract, with one exception.

This acid test should not be applied when speaking to civic clubs. These presentations are usually given at lunch when businesspeople are looking for a little relief from the daily grind. They are more often looking for entertainment and don't want to have to write or work. They just want to sit back and relax. So, if they don't take out paper and pen, don't worry about it.

Examples of simple contracts

What follows are some examples of simple contracts for different speeches in different settings. Try to figure out where and to whom these contracts might apply.

"If you listen and pay heed to the three ideas I'm about to share with you, I guarantee you that the next six months of your life will be the most financially rewarding you have ever experienced. After I'm finished, you will never again have a legitimate reason for earning less than $250,000 a year."

"During the next twenty minutes, I'm going to suggest three specific ways in which you can add a minimum of twenty years to your life. Twenty years is a long time, and I hope you listen closely and begin practicing these principles immediately."

"I urge you to pay close attention to the information I'm about to share with you, because when you leave this room tonight, you will be armed with a specific set of techniques that will radically transform your personal relationships for the better. This may be the most important 15 minutes of your adult life."

"Since we all agreed that increased efficiency is a primary goal, I'll make this guarantee: the three simple suggestions I'm about to give you will improve efficiency by 30 percent within the next week if you apply them to all your work."

Using a contract in a small informal setting

Earlier I talked about how to use Power Speaking principles in a five-minute talk at an informal meeting. I said that you can plan what to say even in those circumstances. You must use a contract then and in fact, it can be even more important. The contract can be short and have an implied message, but it still must be sincere, somewhat exaggerated, and exciting.

Suppose you are at a round-table planning session concerning action to counter legislation proposed by an opposing group. The group is trailing off into irrelevant suppositions, or they are starting to disbelieve the opposing group will really carry through. That often happens in such meetings, because the group starts believing its own arguments against its opposition. They can no longer believe that the opposing group would be stupid enough to continue once confronted with your group's intelligent stand. Of course, this is fantasyland and you know it, and you need to bring the group back to reality. After an opening that could consist of nothing more than a vigorous head shake, which gets your group's attention and says to them, "You're wrong in your supposition," you could say, "They *will* go ahead, I guarantee it."

What is *implied* is: "And if you listen to me for a minute, I will tell you why they will go ahead with their plan, and you will be able to fight them more effectively." It didn't have to be said, and you didn't have the time. It would have been too formal. But the contract was just as strong. I guarantee that if you use similar contracts in all informal or small group settings, you will get the listener's attention.

> *Remember: always make a powerful, excited, and professional contract with the audience. It will be the one thing that can keep you from being amateurish and will establish you as a quality speaker.*

Chapter Review

- The most important part of any speech, talk, or presentation comes after the opening. Typically, it lasts 30 seconds and follows the two-minute opening.

- This part is called a contract with the audience and it is unique to Power Speaking.

- Never tell them what you are going to tell them, tell them, and then tell them what you told them. That's the *worst* piece of advice ever given to would-be Power Speakers.   Use the contract instead.

- In the contract, tell the audience what they will get out of the message.   Use the contract to excite and intrigue listeners, prime them for the message, and let them know they have a good reason to be where they are.

- The contract is *not* a telegraphed encapsulation of the points of the message.

- A contract should use exaggeration within reason, should be sincere and not flippant, and must be exuberant in order to excite the audience.

- One test to determine if the contract is effective is to observe if some audience members take out paper and pen to record what is to be said, except at civic clubs.

- To be the best speaker possible, always use a contract for all occasions.

Chapter 5

Body:
The Next Fifteen Minutes

As I mentioned, *balance* in all speaking assignments is fundamental to Power Speaking principles and must be achieved to ensure success. One way I achieve balance is carefully apportioning time among opening, contract, body, and closing.

Balance is also especially important in the body itself. *Time limit for the body is only 15 minutes.* Most speakers fail when they supply too much information and grow boring during the body of their speeches. Power Speakers, on the other hand, solidify their standing and move listeners with carefully balanced information and supporting elements in the body.

> *The body of any speech must contain no more than three points.*

You're smart. You have a lot to say. You have spent years in your field or have obtained a deep knowledge of a specific vocation. Now you have a chance to tell a group of people about it.

Unfortunately, too much knowledge can ruin a presentation. A novice speaker is tempted to tell the audience everything he knows. Or, while planning his speech, he is faced with an overwhelming amount of knowledge that he wants to include in the text and he becomes confused.

Then, when it comes time to construct the talk, he devises one that contains anywhere from six to twenty points, some overwhelmingly more important than others. Points frequently flow illogically. Major points become subordinated by asides related to minor points, because, though minor, smaller points are often more technical and difficult to understand. By their very nature, minor points require more explanation than major ideas. If all these points are supported thoroughly, the body lasts much more than 15 minutes, and worse, the presentation runs way over the maximum twenty-five minutes and exhausts listeners. When a speaker attempts to use more than three points and sticks to the time limits, some points are submerged. If the speaker only lists all the points at the beginning of the body — a laundry list — listeners count instead of listening.

So, a person who possesses superior knowledge of a subject is often faced with a dilemma: the expertise that makes him a viable speaker and authority figure may also sow the seeds of his own destruction.

Too much knowledge, if not controlled, can be a dangerous thing. Here is an example of what happens. Say you are a top salesman, a big producer year in and year out. Management wants you to share secrets of your success with newer salespeople. You know you must be inspirational and instructional. But you also know the subject so well you can think of a hundred factors behind your success. While constructing your speech, you realize you must include a point about cold calls (a call out of the blue to a potential new client). You want to explain that if a salesman stops cold calling, he is "out of the business," because he must always increase the customer base, if for no other reason than attrition. Fine. This is a major point. But then you think about every other detail in your salesmanship, and they all seem important, too. You think of how your shoes are always polished, how it's a trick of yours to never take in your briefcase on personal visits, how you never call certain clients before noon because that's when they do their paperwork, and so on. You think, "I better tell them about that." Then you come up to another thought: "I also always make a presentation of product on every contact with a client. That's a point I better include, too."

It is very easy to become lengthy and confused. It could happen to any knowledgeable person: the controller telling of cost effectiveness, the company's president telling newcomers of keys to the firm's success.

How does our top producing salesman handle the problem? He starts by understanding his limitations and living with this rule:

The fact is, given the time limit of 15 minutes for the body, you cannot support more than three points. The top producing salesman also understands, as we all must, the listeners' strengths and limitations.

You cannot re-create your world for listeners in 15 minutes. You must rely on the listeners' intelligence. Your job is to stimulate listeners, to give them something to think about and act on, but you have to rely on their ability to fill in the details. If a person in the audience doesn't know about grooming (unless your topic is the importance of good grooming), telling him about a good suit or polished shoes isn't going to help him become a better salesman. Therefore, you must:

Rely on your listeners' ability to project. If the three points are important enough to listeners, if you explain and support points logically, in depth, and with sufficient inspiration, then the audience will be motivated to take the action you suggest. Although you must be clear in explaining points, you must give your listeners some credit for their intellect.

Keeping these facts in mind helps create an atmosphere for limiting the body to three points. However, it still doesn't solve the problem of how to decide which points to use in a 15-minute body when you are an authority on the topic. Here are some suggestions that will help.

Make a list of all the points you can about the topic, both major and minor. Do it fast. Limit the task to 15 minutes or so. Points should come off the top of your head as much as possible. Then walk away and come back an hour later. Some of the major points will jump out at you. They can and should be broad points, the macro issues. Write them down.

Then take a look at what is left on the list. What is left are probably minor points or specifics. Do not throw them away.

Review minor points and consolidate. Assume again that you are the top salesman. Among the minor points remaining are items like: Don't call certain clients immediately before lunch, call them directly after; never tell off-color jokes to some clients; or never let some customers see your Cadillac. Individually, these points aren't very important. Together they mean: know your client. Put it down on the major point list, if you haven't already written it down.

Again, do it fast. If minor points won't consolidate easily, forget them. They aren't important enough for you to waste your time on.

What you have left will be probably be a list of five to ten major points. Now it's judgment time. You will have to examine all your values and decide which three are the most important. More than likely, you will decide quickly on one or two points that must be included. Two or three remaining points will still seem to be of equal importance, and the choices get tougher. There are things you can do to help make a final decision.

Examine the seemingly equal points that remain for their inspirational value. Imagine how you might present them to touch each listener individually. If you still can't decide, then just pick the third point at random.

> *No matter how you decide, do not go over the limit of three points just because the remaining major points seem equally important.*

Once you make the decision, be confident about your choices and don't spend a lot of time second-guessing yourself. By using this process, you will have included at least one or two of the most important points. The others will be so close in value to what you could have included it won't matter. Even though you may have chosen one point at random, it came from a list of very major ideas. Always remember, you know your subject best and, at this point:

> *The success of your presentation now will rest more on how you use information and inspiration to support and explain each major point.*

How to order the points in the body

You must determine which of the three points is more important. Most often, one major idea stands out from the rest. The most important point will be the one that is most inspiring and universal, the one that appeals or can be made to appeal to listeners on an emotional as well as an intellectual level.

> *The major point always comes last in the body.*

How to support each point

What follows are the elements that you *must* include in the speech to support each point. A proper balance is being maintained and the audience is certain to stay focused.

Use each of these four elements to support every point:

1. One humorous anecdote or joke
2. One inspirational story
3. One quote or true incident
4. One how-to

Except for the final point. In the final point, tone down the humor and use *two inspirational stories.*

Limiting the body of the presentation to these elements may seem simple and it is. But the cumulative effect is very balanced, powerful, and polished. Now built around your three major points, the body contains: three good jokes or anecdotes; three important quotes or incidents that are generally accepted truisms or are from people who are either famous, important, or well known to a group or industry; at least three and, perhaps, four touching inspirational stories; and three how-to's. Don't try two jokes for your first point, or two quotes for your second point as that is unbalanced. When you limit yourself to only one of each of the elements to each point, no one point is overshadowed by the other. Jokes do not pile upon jokes, negating the important message.

The audience is not put off with too much inspiration. Each point is perfectly supported. Include general information, facts, and statistics in the elements, and the audience will find you an interesting and exciting speaker.

How to use facts and statistics

Within the context of each major point, limit any facts, statistics, opinions, or other information to the bare essentials. When possible, incorporate supporting data in the content of one of the four elements. Make sure each point gets an equal amount of data. And if, while constructing the speech, you see you're running out of time, always sacrifice facts or other data, rather than one of the four elements.

There is a logical reason for sacrificing facts and subordinating them to stories, quotes, and how-to's. Your authority status as speaker gives listeners the impression you have knowledge that backs up your premise. Too often, speakers ramble on about stats or facts to prove their knowledge. They do this for themselves rather than for the audience.

> *Your purpose as a Power Speaker is to move listeners to action and teach them how to take that action. This is a step beyond information.*

The only data you need to include is to be used to achieve this goal. The four elements are more effective in motivating and teaching than data. Also, there is a natural limitation on the amount of specific information a listener can remember from any presentation. Just as TV news cannot impart as much detail as a newspaper, a speech or talk cannot deliver as much information as a written document. Try it and you will lose listeners because you will be asking them to take in more information than they can possibly digest.

How to arrange the elements within the major points

The particular order in which you use the elements within each point doesn't matter, except that *the how-to's always come at the conclusion of each point.*

However, if you use the same arrangement of elements in each point, the presentation will sound too pat. To make the talk flow naturally, use a different arrangement among the points. If you start off with a joke for the first point, use another element to begin the second, and yet another for the third for variety and smoothness.

When to use this body format

This format for constructing the body to a presentation can be used for all settings without deviation. In fact, many of the nation's leading speakers not only frequently use the same format, but also deliver the exact same speech over and over, with only minor changes. Leo Buscaglia, Norman Vincent Peale, Art Linkletter, and Zig Ziglar have each delivered the same speech thousands of times.

You will be able to do that, too, once you become a professional-quality speaker. Of course, you will only be able to deliver the same speech to different groups. At the beginning, your primary speaking opportunities may be to the same groups, Boards of Directors, civic clubs, salesmen, many different times. And if that is as far as you want to go with speaking, that's fine.

At least you now have only one format to use to prepare your talks. By rearranging elements within each point, the variety is enough to disguise the fact you are using the same format over and over again. The points will be so strong that listeners will focus solely on your message and not the format. So, until you become a professional-quality speaker, never deviate.

How do you know when you are a professional-quality Power Speaker? *When someone is willing to pay you a thousand dollars to speak.*

———————

Chapter Review

- After the contract, the next 15 minutes is the body of your speech.

- The body explores three and only three major points, as it is impossible to support more than three major points in 15 minutes.

- Present the most important point last.

- Support each point by using one of the following:
  1. A humorous anecdote or joke
  2. An inspirational story or illustration
  3. A quote from a famous person, from someone generally known to the group, or of a universally accepted truth
  4. A how-to

Note that this does not apply to the last point. Then tone down humor and two inspirational illustrations are permitted.

- Do not overburden or unbalance the talk with too much data. Data is not as important as the supporting elements.

- The supporting elements are what motivate and teach.

- Vary the arrangement of elements from point to point, but always make the how-to the last element for each point.

- The format can be used for all settings.

- Never deviate from this format until professional quality is attained.

Chapter 6

Review and Closing:
The Final Two Minutes

What you are shooting for, as a Power Speaker, is a standing ovation. It shows that you have captured the listeners' hearts and minds; you have touched them. Of course, a standing ovation is not the sole criteria for judging the success of a presentation. Some occasions and settings, such as a weekly sales meeting or a panel discussion, won't allow it. Perhaps the topic is not the type that could evoke one.

However, your goal should be to try for a standing ovation or its equivalent every time you speak. What do I mean by equivalent of a standing ovation?

Recently, Bob, a Power Speaker, was at one of those informal round-table discussions where he knew he would have only a five to ten minute speaking opportunity. Bob could only guess the exact timing of the opportunity and could, at best, plan the points he thought he would need to make.

Thirty-five bank presidents sat around a large table in a hotel meeting room. They were establishing a new organization to combat impending legislation they believed would destroy their banks.

As he had anticipated, Bob's opportunity came near the end of the discussion, after nearly two hours of crossfire discussion and endless rehashing of points and ideas. As anticipated, the group began to wander and Bob's points had not been made, though they were salient to the issue. He presented his ideas. Because Bob prepared his message using all the Power Speaking techniques, the meeting was brought back into focus, armed now with a very clear and well-defined point. Bob motivated the bankers by concluding with a very strong message of what would happen if they did not take action and how they could take the action. Within ten minutes of the comments, every member decided to continue the fight and to commit thousands of dollars.

It wasn't a standing ovation, but you could consider it the equivalent of one: recognition by the listeners who actively accepted the message.

Every principle of Power Speaking helps you drive your presentation toward this end result: a standing ovation or the equivalent.

The final part of your presentation is the review and closing. While the closing itself cannot assure that you receive a standing ovation, a poorly defined and delivered closing can assure that you won't. As with all the other parts, the closing must be relevant to the rest of the talk and as well planned. Because it is the culmination of all the balanced parts, the closing must be the most powerfully inspiring part of the presentation.

Always end every talk with a powerful inspirational story or statement. *Never* **use humor.** Powerful inspiration in the closing is almost as important as forming a strong contract.

At the largest Positive Thinking rally ever held in Knoxville, Tennessee, several nationally renowned speakers were present to address more than seven thousand listeners. Also present were two speakers who, though not of national importance at that time, were adept professional speakers on the way up.

One used humor as the basis for his speech and ended with a really funny anecdote. This speaker was very good, polished, a real entertainer. The audience laughed and clapped when he was through. The other speaker used inspiration. He made several mistakes in his presentation and, in fact, tended to ramble a bit in the body of his speech. But his closing ended on a touching story of inspiration. The audience jumped to its feet with applause.

The inspirational story or statement you use can be a true story. It can be a provocative supposition or a rhetorical question as in the opening. In one speech, I use a *provocative supposition*. The point is made that several millionaires possess "compassion in the marketplace" as a means of achieving success. I exhort the audience to do likewise. To inspire this action in listeners, the closing thought is: If we all knew the world was going to end in 24 hours, the phone booth's of the planet would be jammed by people calling others to say three magic words: *I love you*. I implore listeners, "Don't wait for the calamity to happen before you make that call."

A supposition like this is always effective because it is a statement that you can create and specifically fit it in with what preceded it. However, a heartwarming story or a true incident can be just as powerful if properly delivered and positioned in the closing.

If an inspirational closing can help achieve that standing ovation, just how do you build a closing? You don't polish off the how-to for point three in the body and then just throw out an inspirational story or idea. The closing must be as balanced as the rest of the speech, with some special attention given to the delivery.

Always begin the closing by tying it back to the opening. *Do not restate the opening.* Only refer to it or restate the conclusion of the opening.

For example, if you use a question like the "five months to live" question, you might begin the closing this way: "Remember when we began, nearly all of you agreed that since you didn't have a five-month guarantee to live, you would make some changes in your lives?"

The original question was not stated; it was only used in reference. The conclusion, drawn by audience and speaker together, is what is restated as a method of review. Doing so wraps the entire presentation into a neat, tight, dynamic package.

After you have reminded the audience of your original premise, then:

Restate the points made in the body. This review is not an endless rehash. Remember, you have only a couple of minutes for the entire closing. What you do is say something like "I've suggested three radical changes you can make to improve your life" (or increase sales or closings, or make better widgets, or grow a healthier flower). Then state the points.

Tell the audience which of the three points is the most important. If you did it correctly, you made the most important of the three points last in the body of your speech.

Now, you will restate the most important point and use it as a transition into your closing inspirational story.

Here is one way to do it. After you restate the three points, say something like "Of these three changes you can make, the third is the most important."

Use the inspirational illustration with a how-to at the end. The illustration you use must be very strong and poignant. It is the culmination of your speech and your last opportunity to move the audience. Just as you support each major point in the body, so must the closing inspiration have a how-to to instruct and exhort the audience. The statement "For God's sake, don't wait for an impending calamity to make that call" implies "do it now." This is a how-to. This is infinitely more moving than a stale joke, isn't it?

How to close: the last words

Never conclude with "thank you." Thank you means as little at the end as it does in the beginning. Likewise, do not say, "It was a pleasure to be here" or "You've been a good audience," or any other fluff.

Try using a warm salutation like "Let's do the best we can," or "We're all in this together," or "You can make a difference." You might even say something like "God bless you" or "May God bless you" and mean it. Use it especially at formal speeches. Without making you sound too much like a preacher, such a phrase conveys a deep sense of feeling and regard for listeners. You can't believe how effective saying that can be in many situations. A heartfelt "God bless you" means something to almost all people; it can take on the nature of a benediction, which usually puts people at ease, with a sense of well-being.

You might not feel comfortable, though, saying, "God bless you" at a weekly sales meeting or a five-minute talk in a round-table discussion (you might still try it occasionally, though; it often works here, if for no other reason than that it is so unexpected). Some phrases you could use to conclude a talk at these settings might be: "Let's get after them," or "Good luck," or "Let's do it right."

Then wait for the standing ovation or the people to corner you. And smile.

Some Tips on Closing

The closing represents a significant break in tone from the body and introduction and, like the contract, requires some special advice to achieve the maximum effect of the closing inspirational thoughts.

Follow the how-to of the last point in the body with a five-to-ten second pause. A pause increases the dramatic effect of what is about to come and gives the members of the audience a chance to catch their breath and collect themselves from the preceding message.

 ♦   **Make direct eye contact with as many in the audience as you can.** During the presentation, you will have been making eye contact. But you may have missed an area of the room. However, as you gain experience, this won't be as much of a problem as it often is at first.

Begin the intent eye contact at the pause and continue, as if searching, throughout your closing.

 ♦   **Significantly lower your voice.** Significantly lowering your voice, as a dramatic break from the prior level, increases the intensity of the moment and makes listeners intent on hearing the final words. The change assures their attention. If you don't believe it, try this during a telephone conversation: when you get to a very important point in the conversation, start whispering. Tell the person on the other phone that you don't want someone near to hear you. You'll find every time that the other person will start to whisper, too. The effect is that you are sharing, very personally, a special concept or secret.

 ♦   **Reduce the speed of delivery by as much as two-thirds.** This also increases the drama and importance of your final thought. Your radical shift in rate lets the audience know it is now receiving the most important message.

———————

Chapter Review

The final two minutes of a speech are the review and closing. The following applies:

- Every Power Speaker's goal is to receive a standing ovation or its equivalent.

- To achieve a standing ovation, use inspiration. Never use humor in the closing.

- Inspiration can be a true story or a provocative supposition.

- Always tie the first comments of the closing back to the introduction.

- Next, restate the three points covered in the body.

- Restate the third, most important point and use it as a transition into the inspirational element.

- Deliver the inspirational illustration.

- Tie a how-to directly to the end of the illustration.

- Final words should be "God bless you" or something similar in formal speeches. For less formal settings, say "Good luck" or something similar. Never close with "Thank you" or "It was a pleasure being here."

- Vary the delivery of the closing from the rest of the speech in these ways:

  1. Pause five to ten seconds after completing the last how-to of the last point in the body.
  2. Make direct eye contact with as many in the room as possible, starting with the pause and continuing through the entire closing.

3. Significantly lower the volume of your voice.
4. Slow down the delivery rate by as much as two-thirds.

Chapter 7
Gestures and Conduct

Gestures in Power Speaking mean *everything* you do in your mannerisms, not just a few arm and hand movements tied to the speech, from the minute you approach the podium until you sit down after your standing ovation. I include conduct with gestures because the entire manner in which you handle yourself is critical to being a successful Power Speaker.

If you are truly excited about your speech and deliver it with enthusiasm, your arm and hand movements will reflect that. Maintaining an attitude of drama and enthusiasm throughout the presentation will make you animated. Your hands and arms will wave around. You will reach out to the crowd. You will use those gestures that come naturally to you as a result of the enthusiasm you have about your presentation and the very dynamic message you have prepared.

Keep in mind that you want to exude confidence and poise, while being natural and at ease. You can't do that if you are worried about memorizing four hundred gestures for a twenty-five minute talk. You certainly wouldn't do that for a five-minute informal discussion, would you?

However, there are a few gestures you can use that help establish your status as an authority and help put you and the audience at ease.

Always wear a wristwatch and take it off, glance at it, and place it on the lectern. Calmly, deliberately, and slowly rise from your chair (this is obviously for formal speeches) and slowly walk to the podium. You are in control. Pause for a look at the audience. Then slip off your watch, give it a quick look, and place it on the podium.

In its own way, doing this makes a subtle contract with the audience. Even if you don't actually note the time, which you won't, you are giving the audience a dramatic indication that you are concerned about their time. The action implies you are not about to go beyond the allotted time period. You should even do this for short talks.

Walk away from notes at regular intervals. Walking away from your notes, away from the lectern, does several things for you. It helps loosen you up so it is easier for you to be yourself and to become animated and excited. Walking away from notes provides variety for the audience. You help your own confidence and comfort and you will also maintain the attention of your listeners.

Speakers who just stand in one place, behind the lectern, are almost always boring, and they exude no confidence in themselves. You don't want to be in that position. One suggestion is to walk away from the notes *no fewer than eight to ten times during the presentation.*

Here is something very important for you to know about walking away from notes. You need a microphone that will allow you to do it. Never accept a speaking engagement where you are confined to the podium or where you are not allowed to walk around.

As you become involved more in public speaking, you'll discover that you are in the driver's seat when it comes to the type of equipment you need. Just tell the person who books you that you need a microphone that will allow you to move around.

What about smaller meetings or round tables? It depends on whether you are standing before the group or sitting at a desk or table. If standing, by all means move. Perhaps five to seven times. If sitting, at least shift your chair, lean forward and back, from time to time.

Make eye contact with as many in the room as possible. The best way for you to establish personal contact with your listeners is to make direct eye contact with as many people as you can. This not only shows you are in control of yourself and the material, but it also indicates your confidence and sincerity.

Even though you know inherently that you should be looking each person squarely in the eye, you have to force yourself to make eye contact. During a twenty-five minute presentation, you can meet most people's eyes. In smaller, informal settings, do it with everyone.

And don't try to get by with the old cheap trick of looking over people's heads to a point at the back of the room or at the tops of listeners' heads. That's a silly notion that supposedly allows you to overcome fear. The audience knows you are doing it, and it only diverts their attention and detracts from your authority.

Pause after humor and inspiration. In public speaking, the only thing painful about quiet is that it tends to be scary for the speaker. Don't let it scare you. Use it to your advantage to collect yourself and stay in control. You can be quiet all you want, because you are the person in front of everyone, in control of the situation.

Pauses are very good for the audience, too, and they like them. Pauses give listeners a chance to catch their breath and to digest what you have just said.

A good pause following an inspirational story gives the message more impact by setting it off from the speech. It acts like a period at the end of a sentence.

You want to pause after humor to let any laughter die down. The laughter of just one person will trample over the next few words of the message for everyone else at the table or even in the whole room.

Now, when I say *pause* after humor and inspiration, I mean pause. Total silence. Don't say another word. This silence should last for about three to five seconds, unless there is laughter. In that case, let it die out.

Speak fast — about 350 words per minute. As you become an adept Power Speaker, you learn to make your presentations jam-packed with wonderful ideas, stories, and inspiration. Often the only way to get these necessary and moving ideas into the allotted time is with a rapid delivery. Too frequently, the people who speak at the traditional slow 170 word-per-minute pace are only doing so because they really have little to say. Not you; you will have so much to say, you won't be able to contain yourself.

The way to increase speed is with practice. Each time you practice, try to pick up the pace. As you come to know your anecdotes and stories better, you will naturally tell them with ease and excitement, just as you do when telling stories to friends.

Don't be afraid to try it. If someone tells you after a talk that you speak too fast, take it as one of the best compliments you can get. Just this one note: don't forget to slow down during the closing.

Never point to the audience unless you are explaining or emphasizing a positive fact. For some reason, people are programmed to respond when someone points, if not actively, then subconsciously. The act of pointing will inadvertently emphasize or call attention to words or phrases you are saying at the time. Therefore, never use pointing unless there is some positive fact or material you want listeners to get or feel on a subconscious level. If you have a habit of pointing, break it.

Never carry any extra objects to the podium. Other than your notes or the watch that you lay down, don't take anything. That especially means a pen. Invariably, when you take a pen with you, you fiddle with it. That's distracting for the audience. Everyone in the audience will watch the object and completely ignore what's said. If you don't believe it, check the next time you see a TV anchor or newscaster who has a pen in hand. You won't know anything about the stories being reported.

Never excuse yourself for any reason. Never excuse yourself for a burp, sneeze, or glitch. Why in the world would you want to draw attention to a mistake? Let me assure you that if you are speaking with amplification, everybody heard it. By the rare miracle that someone didn't notice, his reaction to your apology will be "Oh, did he goof?" As it is, the cough, hack, or stutter was enough diversion without your dragging it out. Besides, you can't accomplish anything by asking for the audience to excuse you. Imagine your surprise if the audience jumped up en masse and said, "You're excused!"

Never rest your weight on one foot, lean on the podium with your elbow, or put hands in your pocket. These are slovenly, slouchy things to do. They indicate you have little interest in your presentation or the audience.

Never eat less than an hour before your presentation. Never eat at the meeting where you are going to speak. Aside from the obvious concern of spilling food on yourself, there are more important reasons to avoid food.

One reason is that when you eat, blood circulates to your stomach to help digest food. The brain is left with a lower blood supply and this is the reason people always feel like taking a nap after a big meal. If you eat less than an hour before you speak, you simply aren't as sharp and you have a far greater chance of losing your quick wit and finely honed presentation skills.

You also risk the chance of getting food caught in your throat, increase chances of burping, or chance heartburn.

A note on water: it's okay to have water at the podium. Try not to drink it, but have it for emergencies.

Chapter Review

In Power Speaking, gestures refer to every movement made during a presentation. The following applies with respect to gestures and overall attitude as a Power Speaker:

* Hand and arm movements must be natural. If you're excited and enthusiastic about the presentation, hand and arm movements come naturally.

* Natural instincts keep most people from being out of control with their arm or hand movements.

* Always wear a wristwatch. Take it off, glance at it, and place it on the lectern. Do this after the opening pause, but well before starting to speak. Using the wristwatch forms a subtle contract with listeners that the speaker is aware of their precious time.

* Walk away from notes at least eight to ten times during the presentation. It helps speakers loosen up, provides variety for listeners, and shows who's in command.

* Make sure proper equipment is available for movement away from notes well before the presentation. Use a clip microphone or a cordless microphone.

* Make direct eye contact with as many in the room as possible. Never try to squelch fear by looking over listeners' heads or at a point in the back of the room.

◆ Speak fast. Try to speak at about 350 words per minute.

◆ Never point unless you are emphasizing a positive point that you want the audience to feel on a subconscious level.

◆ Always pause after inspiration for about five seconds and until laughter dies down after humor. Laughter will drown out the next few words if there is no pause. After inspiration a pause is dramatic. Never be afraid of silence; use it to your advantage.

◆ Never carry any extra objects to the podium.

◆ Never make excuses for any reason.

◆ Never rest weight on one leg, rest an elbow on the lectern, or put hands in pockets.

◆ Don't eat less than an hour before the presentation. After eating, blood rushes to the stomach and makes you drowsy. Also, there's the risk of becoming sick.

Chapter 8

Practical Application and Sample Speech

It's time to look at a practical application of the principles I've presented. What follows is a sample speech with a running analysis. Included is an example of the specific outline for this speech as it is used before an audience and a general outline.

The speech I am using is not merely a sample. I have delivered this particular speech over 500 times to more than 500 diverse groups, from a graduating class of nurses of the nursing school at the University of Texas to a group of auto body and fendermen at Maaco's annual convention. The speech seldom fails to evoke a standing ovation. It is practical and proven.

What I want you to do with the speech is study how all the parts fit together, keeping in mind your needs as you go along. Take note of how the transitions from one point to the next make the speech smooth and coherent. As you go through the speech, you might want to stop and consider how you would plug in elements for a topic you have been considering.

A sidelight of this sample is that you can see how a broadly defined inspirational speech can be delivered to a wide range of groups. Of course, you may not want to do that kind of speech. I only use this speech to show how a speech with broad appeal can work. The same principles at work in a speech of mass appeal also work with power for narrower topics. *Inspiration and balance* are the ingredients necessary for your success.

The speech

A note on how to read the speech: this is the exact transcription of a speech. It will not be as grammatically correct as the written word.   This speech was not read but delivered from outline notes, as all speeches must be.

You might wish to read it aloud, trying to decide where you think pauses, or dramatic emphasis, should be (might as well practice a presentation now).

One other note. Each time I delivered this speech, the fee was about a thousand dollars. Not bad for twenty minutes work, is it?

I. Opening

"Ladies and gentlemen, if you knew you had only a five-month guarantee to live, how many of you would immediately change parts of your life?

"Now, before raising your hands, let me rephrase that question so you fully understand it. What if you went to a physician and he told you that you had terminal cancer, and he told you that you had only five months to live.   And then you went to a second physician who confirmed the diagnosis of the first one, and he too said that you had only a five-month guarantee.

"If you would change something about your life — perhaps the way you treat your family, friends, associates. . . maybe you would quit your job. . . perhaps you would travel . . . .   If you had only a five-month guarantee and you would make definite changes in your life — would you all please raise your hands?

"Please put your hands down. Now for a more sobering question. Those of you who have a five-month guarantee from right now, would you please raise your hands?

"Obviously, ladies and gentlemen, most of you have changes you should make in your life, especially now that we understand that you don't have a guarantee. Today, I want to suggest some changes that you can make that will radically change your life in a short time.

"Recently, I was privileged to work with a team of writers for a major business periodical. Our purpose was to write an article that was different about ten multimillionaires. We were to go out and find ten people who were multimillionaires and totally self-made. We were to try and uncover if there were two or three qualities unique to the millionaires that had not been carefully studied but should be written about for the general public.

"We found, as we interviewed these millionaires, that there were some qualities in common among all of them that business periodicals had overlooked.

II. Contract

"The three qualities that these millionaires shared, and frankly, qualities that you can incorporate immediately to change your lives are:

Number one: the ability to focus on perspectives beyond;

Number two: positive imagery; and

Number three: compassion.

"I can guarantee you that if you take these qualities — begin applying them immediately to your own life — if you will make these changes beginning today, you will see a tremendous change in your income in a very, very short time.

III. Body
A. First Point

"You will recall that the first quality of these millionaires that will help you change your life was literally the ability to focus on perspectives beyond.

What I mean by that is, things are not as they appear to be. And most of these millionaires learned to see beyond the outer appearances that would slow down most people and indicate negativity.

"I went to college in a state where they have volunteer fire departments. And at one time, there was a fire that took place at a large oil refinery that rested at the bottom of a hill. The heat was so intense that the arriving volunteer fire chiefs had decided that they could not go down to the bottom of the hill and put out the fire, and that it would eventually burn itself out anyway.

"The media were all there. The fire had been raging for some thirty minutes when all of a sudden, in the distance, there came the clanging bell of a small volunteer fire truck. It was very picturesque. An old fire chief, men hanging on for dear life, even a Dalmatian.

"As the fire truck neared the crowd that always gathers at these things, it became apparent to everyone that it wasn't going to stop. So the crowd parted, the fire truck rolled right down to the bottom of the hill, circled the fire a couple of times, the men jumped off and started fighting the fire.

"When the blaze of this raging fire had been fought for a few minutes by this small volunteer fire department, it became apparent that they were putting the fire out. So, spurred to heroism, all the other volunteer fire departments rushed down to fight the fire, and indeed it was out in an hour.

"Now, the way that they finance these volunteer fire departments in this state is by taking up a collection right at the scene of the blaze, which is practical—men risking life and limb is motivational to crowds. So they took up a collection at this fire and collected eighteen hundred dollars. The crowd concluded that they ought to give all the eighteen hundred dollars to this old fire chief from this small town because due to his heroism the others had joined in.

"And so, as the weary firefighters crested the top of the hill, the six o'clock news reporter moved in with his mini-cam, the newspaper reporters moved in, and they surrounded this old fire chief from this small community. The TV reporter said, 'You know, due to your act of bravery, everybody here, all the fire people, rushed down and helped put out the fire.   We collected eighteen hundred dollars.   We want you to have all the money. Tell us, Mr. Fire Chief, what are you going to do with all eighteen hundred dollars?'

"And the ruddy-faced old fire chief wiped the sweat off his brow and spit a plug of tobacco on the ground and said, 'Well, sir, the first thing I'm going to do is fix the brakes on that damn truck!'

"You see, things aren't always as they appear to be. And these millionaires understood that and were able to see beyond outer appearances.

"I was called a Houdinologist in college because of my avid love of the life of Houdini and studying how he lived.

"Houdini was invited, at the height of his career, to break out of a bank vault in Europe, which the owners of the new bank had said was totally impenetrable. And, of course, when Houdini found out that all the press was going to be there, he agreed to the escape attempt.

"Now, there are a couple of things you need to know about Houdini, in case you don't. He had two requirements at every one of these attempts. One was that he be allowed to kiss his wife. The other was that they drop a curtain in front of him so that nobody could see how he actually performed his feats.

"The key to Houdini's effectiveness was that his wife would frequently pass a wire from her mouth to his as they kissed, and then, of course, Houdini was a master lock picker and he would simply extract the wire from his mouth once they dropped the curtain and he could get into or out of virtually any situation.

"Well, on this particular occasion of the grand opening of the bank in London, the press was all there, and Houdini had agreed to break out in under three minutes as long as he was allowed to kiss his wife and they would drop a curtain. The curtain was in place, the press was ready, Houdini kissed his wife and entered the bank vault, they dropped the curtain and he immediately pulled out the wire and began picking the lock on this massive bank vault.

"He later wrote in his memoirs that after the first minute, he had heard none of the familiar clicking sounds.

"After the second minute, he was beginning to sweat profusely, realizing that if he didn't pull it off, his career was in jeopardy.

"After two minutes and forty-five seconds, he reached into his pocket to wipe the sweat from his brow, and as he did so, he inadvertently leaned against the bank vault door and it creaked open.

"You see, the door had never been locked, except in Houdini's mind.

"And I submit to you today, that as these multimillionaires understood, you must begin to change your perspectives on life to understand that the only limitations you will ever experience, the only locked doors, the only things that keep you away from the success you feel you deserve, are literally self-imposed limitations, as in the Houdini example.

"So remember the Houdini story.   But there's another thing you need to know about.

"My favorite holiday is Halloween.   And the reason for that is, as I understand the origin of Halloween, it began with the old Druids in England centuries ago, and later was called All Hallows' Day. They partied, as do our children; they wore masks and costumes, all day long.   This was the adults who participated, not just children.   However, there was a remarkable difference between All Hallows' Day and the current Halloween.

"And the difference was, at midnight on All Hallows' Day, all the adults took off their masks and their costumes, and the new holiday was begun.   And the new holiday was All Saints' Day.   Because, you see, even those ancient people way back in London understood the fact that underneath all the masks and facades and games we adults play, there really is, at the core of all of us, a living saint.

"And I can assure you, these multimillionaires demonstrate that the cream always rises to the top. Because they were capable of seeing beyond the masks of not only their peers and associates and subordinates, but also their competitors and the people with whom they did business. All the millionaires, without exception, pointed out in some way that they could see the saint and the loveliness in every single other human being.

"A beautiful example of the ability to focus on perspectives beyond.

"Remember, one of the key abilities is the ability to focus on perspectives beyond. How do we do this? Very simple. I want each of you to remember the Depression from now on whenever any limiting situation arises in your life.

"Never before in the history of the planet, and certainly in the Free World, has there ever been a period in which so many people killed themselves who were successful, and so many people who were impoverished became multimillionaires.

"Now, the circumstances were all the same. The only difference between the people who went out of windows and the people who became multimillionaires was their focus. So from now on, when events or situations or individuals come up in your life that cause you all manner of difficulty, let a little red flag go up in your mind that is waving and saying the word *Depression*. And remember that your choice of focus as to the nature of the event you're encountering will literally result in the outcome. You, like these millionaires, will either go into a suicidal mode, as they did during the Depression or, as the impoverished people who could see the good behind all negativity, you will emerge victorious.

"So, remember the Depression and always focus on the idea that your limited thinking is unnecessary when negative situations occur, and that will enable you, like these millionaires, to create the ability to focus on perspectives beyond.

B. Second Point

"The second quality of these millionaires, and a second change you can make in your life to make it more meaningful, is simply: positive imagery.

"I used to own a car dealership in a small community in the Midwest. And one weekend a young man named Steve came to me right out of the military, who had never sold anything.

"And Steve asked if he could become a salesman. Although he had no practical experience and didn't even have a high school diploma, he was such a nice young fellow and had such a darling family, I agreed to put him to work. I began by putting him through all the General Motors training films on handling objections and closing sales. The first month, Steve only sold two cars. One car and one truck, to be specific.

"He came to me at the end of the month and he said, 'Please don't fire me. I definitely believe I can be a salesman.'

"At that point, I said, 'You know, Steve, some people aren't cut out for this job, but would you do anything I told you? Would you take my word and advice that there is a system that will help you?'

"Steve said, 'I would do anything. But please don't fire me; just give me one more month.'

"So I took Steve in the office and I had him pull out a business card and I said, 'Steve what I want you to do is number the back of that little card from one to five.' Which he then did. I said, 'Now, Steve, write down the five things you want most out of life over the next thirty days. And one of the things I want you to write down is to sell thirty cars or trucks.'

"He laughed at me, and I said, 'Steve, you said you'd do anything.' So he began writing.

"One of his objectives he wrote down on the back of his card was to sell thirty cars. After he made his list of five, I said, 'Now, Steve, what I want you to do is sit down three times a day, close your eyes, and vividly imagine yourself in those sets of circumstances.' Which he agreed to do. And I said, "Steve, if you sell the thirty cars and trucks, at the end of the month, I'll buy you the most expensive pair of cowboy boots you can find anywhere.' He laughed and ambled out of the office.

"That month, Steve sold twenty-eight cars and trucks. I bought him the boots anyway. And there's a small community right now in Oklahoma where you can walk in and see his name on the sign as owner of this dealership.

"If you walk into Steve's office, and ask him how he was able to accomplish ownership of a dealership in only five years, without high school or college degrees, he will pull out a tattered business card, and share with you the system I just told you about.

"So you see, positive imagery is one of the qualities that these millionaires talked about. The ability, as Steve learned, to creatively visualize themselves in circumstances in which they really wish to find themselves at a later date.

"It kind of reminds me of the story of Jesus Christ and Moses.

"Jesus and Moses were in heaven one day discussing the fact that it was lamentable that they had never played golf. Jesus brought it up first. He said, 'I wish we had lived in the twentieth century because I've watched Arnold Palmer play golf and it looks like a lot of fun.'

"And Moses said, 'You know, we can do anything we want. Let's go back to Earth for a little while and play eighteen holes.'

"Jesus said, 'Okay, let's do it.'

"So, they manifested themselves on a beautiful golf course at La Jolla. They were in golf clothes. Jesus said, 'You know, Moses, I want to go first. I want to tee up my ball. If Arnold Palmer can do it, I can do it.'

"Moses said, 'Be my guest.'

"So Jesus teed up the ball. Took a driver. Made a beautiful swing and drove the ball 200 yards right into the middle of a water trap, a large lake. Frustratedly,

Jesus shrugged his shoulders and said, 'I don't understand it. If Arnold Palmer can do it, I can do it.' With that, he ran out to the edge of the water, looked around to make sure no one was observing him, walked out onto the water, got his ball, and ran back.

"He said to Moses, 'I'm going to tee it up again. If Arnold Palmer can do it, I can do it.'

"Again, he teed the ball. Again, he took a marvelous swing, this time driving the ball 250 yards. Again, the ball went into the water.

"Now, he was frustrated. He said, 'Moses, I don't understand it. If Arnold Palmer can do it, I can do it.'

"Again, he went running to the edge of the water, looked both ways, walked out onto the water quickly, reached down, got his ball.

"Well, there were some gentlemen in the clubhouse having some drinks, watching this activity. And they were so amazed, they went out to tee box. One of them went up to Moses and tugged on his sleeve. When he had his attention, he said, 'Hey, buddy, who does your friend think he is, Jesus Christ?'

"Moses said, 'No, Arnold Palmer.'

"So, I'm not advocating that you necessarily visualize things about yourself that aren't true. But I am saying creative visualization and positive imagery are essential.

"Ladies and gentlemen, positive imagery was not only prevalent among these millionaires.

"I know of people who aren't multimillionaires who have used positive imagery in a very powerful way.

"For example, I once met this woman named Frances, a single black mother, who single-handedly built a very successful temporary employment company from scratch in Los Angeles. In fact, she had literally started from her garage with a few inexpensive business machines she bought from the local pawn shop, and parlayed this into a multimillion dollar venture. Anyway, here is this woman who when growing up was all but neglected by the education system because she was considered mildly retarded and unable to learn.   No matter what anyone tried, she simply could not read.

"This went on until Frances was into her teens and finally one day, she was watching TV on a Sunday morning and happened to see Robert Schuller during his Hour of Power sermon. He was talking about the power of positive thinking. This teaching captivated her. In fact, it was through Schuller that Frances learned about the power of positive imagery. She learned that by determining in her mind that she could achieve something she could actually go out and achieve it! Well, of course, the first thing she wanted more than anything was to be able to read. So she began to imagine herself reading. In a matter of months, Frances not only taught herself to read, but she excelled to the point that she could read at a level exceeding that of others her age!

"Years later, Frances was faced with another great challenge. This time, she had two children and her husband had left her. This was the first time that she had not only had to provide for herself, but she had to provide for her two children as well. After several months of struggle and living on welfare, Frances decided that this was not the life she wanted for herself or her children. So, she decided to set a goal for herself: to start her own business. Again, just as she did before to succeed, she used positive imagery in this situation. Frances imagined herself in an office building with people working for her as she ran a company of her own. At first she wasn't even sure what the business would be. But from that point on, within three years, she had built her successful temporary employment company. She now teaches others how to apply positive imagery in their own lives.

"Frances is just another example of people who have learned the power of positive imagery.

"You see, these millionaires weren't the only ones to use this, but also average people in everyday lives can do a multitude of wonderful things.

"How do you excel at positive imagery?

"The same way that Steve did in the automobile dealership illustration earlier.

"I suggest you take out a business card and begin practicing the imagery process three times a day. Most of the millionaires had the same system and followed the same format.

"So, please, when this speech is concluded, either this evening or tomorrow, in the privacy of your own office or home, take out a business card, make a list of the things you want more than anything in the world, and then practice daily seeing yourself in those sets of circumstances. Imagine them vividly, as if they had already happened, and then cross things off as they come true in your life.

"What you'll soon discover, as these millionaires did, is you'll be changing your business card almost weekly, as new and exciting things come into your life based on your positive imagery capabilities.

"Don't believe me. Try it.

C. Third Point

"The third quality that all the millionaires interviewed had in common was their ability to be compassionate.

"When I was in seminary, Eddie Edwards, one of my classmates who had been a CPA and had decided to go into the ministry, told us a story that I shall never forget. It changed all our lives.

"He said, 'When I was five years old, my father died and my mother, believing that she could not financially afford to raise us, took us to an orphanage.'

"Eddie said, 'Though I was only seven, I can remember how I broke away from that stern woman at the orphanage and chased the taxicab in which my mother was riding. She was waving a handkerchief in the back window and crying. And I remember shouting at the top of my little lungs, 'Mommy, I hate you, and I'll never forgive you.' Well, I'm forty-five now. And as I was preparing to become ordained as a Christian minister, I had an unnerving feeling that I really had something wrong in my life.   And finally after much prayerful consideration I realized what it was.'

"Eddie was telling us this at the final chapel service before we were to be ordained.

"He said, 'I went to a telephone two weeks ago, I had done some research prior to that, and I picked up the phone and I dialed a number in Bellingham, Washington, and when a little old lady answered the phone, I said, 'Hi, Mom. This is Eddie. I love you and I forgive you.'

"Eddie told us, 'My friends, I have been chasing that taxicab for forty years and I finally caught it.'

"I don't know what taxicabs you're chasing, but I do know that all those millionaires recognized the importance of showing compassion for your competitors, your peers, your associates, your family — everybody with whom you come in contact.   Because you see, compassion may just be the greatest tool in free enterprise because it's utilized by so few.

"When I was working my way through seminary, I was a used car salesman.   In fact, many of my classmates put up a picture of me in the student lounge, and under it they put the caption, 'Would you buy a used God from this man?'   At any rate, I sold thirty cars one month working part time.

"And the boss, Boots Williams, as was the custom, invited me to speak to all the salespeople Monday morning because I was the leader.   I remember telling him, 'No, Boots, you don't want me to tell the truth about what I really do because people will laugh and make fun of me.'

"He said, 'I don't care what they do.   I want you to conduct the sales meeting on Monday and I want you to tell your secrets of sales success.   You're only working part time and you outsold my other people who all are working full time.'

"So, I agreed.

"Monday morning, I stood before all the salespeople at Boots Williams Ford in Kansas City. There were thirty-five of them.

"As I stood there and began, I simply glanced out at my audience of bleary-eyed, half-hungover people and said, 'You know, when somebody walks onto the car lot, I think, 'If I can sell you a car at a price you can afford, I hope I do so. But oh, God, let me understand the situation these people are in so I don't push them. And that's how I sell a lot of cars. I feel compassion for people.'

"Well, of course, you could imagine that these salespeople stared at me as if I were crazy. But I can assure you, without exception, within the next week, when everybody knew that no one else was watching, one at a time, they would grab me, take me aside, and say, 'Hey, teach me about compassion.'

"You see, compassion works. And if you were to go into Boots Williams Ford and ask him how they went from number twenty-seven to number three in the whole Kansas City zone, Boots Williams would tell you about compassion for the customer.

"And I'm talking about compassion for everyone, even our competitors. I remember once I was standing in the lobby of the Hilton in San Francisco making a call at a phone bank there just before a speaking engagement at a conference. And as I was on the phone, I noticed an unusually tall man strolling towards the men's room just across from me. I probably would not have taken notice of him at all if he had not been such a tall, solidly built man and had he not looked very much like a speaker I had seen in flyers and posters around the conference. As he passed me, I looked only briefly at him and immediately directed my attention to the phone call I was making.

"Then, several minutes later, after I had just concluded my phone call and was about to head to the banquet room where I was to make my speech, the same man exited the men's room. Only this time, I noticed a streamer of toilet paper running from the back of his pants, trailing about six feet behind. 'Good grief,' I thought, 'This poor man could look awfully foolish if he doesn't take care of this right away.' So many times most people may see something like this, chuckle to themselves and go on. But, because of the compassion I had for this man, I simply had to call attention to his toilet paper stream. In fact, I knew that from where we were, I could keep this from being a public spectacle by mentioning it immediately. Which I did. He was immensely grateful, though still fairly embarrassed. After a few moments of laughter, he introduced himself to me. It turned out that I was right; this man was a very capable speaker quickly becoming popular on the lecture circuit. We later got to know each other and have been good friends ever since. Moreover, through him, I have actually been given some excellent referrals for speaking engagements, yielding a great deal of money.

"I'm talking about compassion. I suppose the best illustration I could ever hope to draw on is found in a book by a wonderful surgeon from New Haven, Connecticut. The title of the book is *Mortal Lessons*. The doctor's name is Richard Seizer. And no other illustration in any other book I've ever read, or any other story I've heard in real life, is so full of compassion. I'd like to read you a section from this book. It's found on page forty-five of *Mortal Lessons*, by Richard Seizer.

"I stand by the bed where a young woman lies, her face postoperative, her mouth twisted in a palsy, clownish. A tiny twig of the facial nerve, the one to the muscles of her mouth has been severed. She will be thus from now on. The surgeon had followed with religious fervor the curve of her flesh; I promise you that. Nevertheless, to remove the tumor in her cheek, I had to cut the little nerve.

"Her young husband is in the room. He stands on the opposite side of the bed, and together they seem to dwell in the evening lamplight, isolated from me, private. Who are they, I ask myself, he and this wry-mouth I have made, who gaze at each other so generously, greedily? The young woman speaks.

"'Will my mouth always be like this?' She asks.

"'Yes,' I say. 'It will. It is because the nerve was cut.'

"She nods, and is silent. But the young man smiles.

"'I like it,' he says. 'It's kind of cute.'

"All at once, I *know* who he is. I understand and I lower my gaze. One is not bold in an encounter with a god. Unmindful, he bends to kiss her crooked mouth, and I so close I can see how he twists his own lips to accommodate to hers, to show her that their kiss still works. I remember that the gods appeared in ancient Greece as mortals, and I hold my breath and let the wonder in.

"Now isn't that a powerful example of compassion? And I can assure you that all of these millionaires, without exception, suggested to us that they used principles of compassion — even with their competitors.

"How do you do that?

"The next time you're involved in any human interaction, place yourself in someone else's situation. You don't have to tell them. You don't have to let them know what you're doing. Just know that when you feel compassion for someone else, you are closer to understanding them and moving them to a particular action you may want, i.e., selling a car or whatever.

IV. Closing

"So there you have it. Three qualities that are critical. Three changes that you can make, especially in view of the fact that you don't have a five-month guarantee. And without exception, you all agreed you'd make changes if you did.

"Those three changes, those three qualities of the millionaires: the ability to focus on perspectives beyond; positive imagery; and compassion.

"And probably of all three, the last one is the most important. Because, ladies and gentlemen, I can make you one guarantee, and that is this:

"If all of a sudden every man, woman, and child alive on planet earth today were suddenly, simultaneously to discover that this earth was going to destroy itself, or be destroyed within the next twenty-four hours, the phone booths of the planet would be literally packed with people just like you and me; feverishly fumbling for a quarter to call another human being in another place and say three magic words — I. Love. You. Don't wait for a catastrophe. Do it now.

"God bless you."

Sample outline of a speech

This speech was not read but delivered from outline notes, which were written on three-by-five index cards. Here is the outline for the speech as it was delivered. Your outline notes don't have to be a perfect literary outline.

I. Five Months to Live Question

II. Article About Ten Millionaires
A. Three Qualities You Can Accept to Change Lives
1. The Ability to Focus on Perspectives Beyond
2. Positive Imagery
3. Compassion
B. Guaranteed to Change Your Life, Financially

III. The Ability to Focus on Perspectives Beyond
A. Fire Truck Story
B. Houdini Story
C. Halloween and All Saints' Day
        Removing of masks and saints within
D. Remembering the Depression
        Millionaires and suicide, poverty and success

IV. Positive Imagery
A. Car Sales Story (Steve)
B. Jesus, Moses, Arnold Palmer and Golf Story
C. Frances' Story
D. Write Desires on Back of Business Card as Steve Did

V. Compassion
A. Eddie Edwards Story
B. Boots Williams
      Used cars and seminary
C. Toilet paper story
D. *Mortal Lessons* Passage; Dr. Richard Seizer, page 45
E. Meaning of Compassion

VI. Most Important: Compassion
A. Phone Booth Story
B. Do It Now

Here is an example of a general outline that you could follow as you construct and practice your speech.

OPENING: Two minutes

I. Opening rhetorical question

CONTRACT: Thirty seconds to a minute and a half

II. Contract (or Optional)
A. Three points
      1. Point one
      2. Point two
      3. Point three
B. Contractual statement

BODY: Fifteen minutes

III. Point One
A. Humor
B. Quote or true incident
C. Inspiration
D. How-to

IV. Point Two
A. Quote or true incident
B. Humor
C. Inspiration
D. How-to

V. Point Three
A. Inspiration
B. Quote or true incident
C. Humor
D. Inspiration
E. How-to

CLOSING: Two minutes

VI. Closing
A. Conclusion of opening
B. Review statement of points
C. Inspiration
D. How-to

Chapter 9
Where to Get Inspiration

Inspiration is what draws a crowd to you; it is what people are searching for. You must use inspiration in every speech, talk, or presentation you make before groups. Inspiration is more important than humor and statistics. It will solidify your position as an authority more quickly and more convincingly than any other facet of speaking, or any other type of communication for that matter, because it indicates that you have deep insight into the realities of life and that you are willing to share that insight.

If you have a message to give, a point you believe you must get across, you can write down and hand out all the statistical data you want. But the conclusion and what it means to each individual can only be provided by your inspiration. It provides a reason for changes and moves people to the point of accepting your ideas on how to accomplish change.

Although the principles of Power Speaking advocate radical departures from past concepts on public speaking such as a contract, a balanced approach, a limited format, etc., *the real difference that makes these principles powerful is the absolute reliance on inspiration in all settings.*

The challenge of finding inspiration

The problem for you is where and how do you get the inspirational stories and illustrations you need?

Surprisingly, the people who intend to use Power Speaking in a business setting, at their local civic clubs, or before professional associations, but never on a speaking tour, must keep digging for inspirational stories, more than do professional speakers on tour.

That's odd, isn't it? The people who get paid $1,000 to $10,000 for after-dinner speeches don't have to work as hard to get their inspiration as do the people who stay "in-house." That's because the pro speaker can recycle a speech to different audiences. Pros can be more selective because they don't have to change a story unless a better, more illustrative one comes along, or until they hit a familiar group a second time. And even then they don't often change because they assume a good story last year is a good story this year, too.

When you have to speak to the same group over and over again, you have to come up with new stories. However, finding these stories will be a valuable vehicle for you to get all those raises, promotions — that rise to the top — that I talked about.

What I provide here are some unique ways to get good, usable, powerful, inspirational illustrations. Keep this in mind as you read some of these unusual ways of finding inspiration: Some *are* unorthodox. In Power Speaking, I do things that others have never dreamed of doing.

Always carry a pen and pad with you to record your observations of life. Power Speakers must be "tuned in" to life, but it is even more important for you to record the keenness of your observations. As many inspirational stories arise from personal observations of life as come from books or research. More important, these stories are often the best stories because they reveal the genuineness and closeness of immediate observation, key to powerful inspiration.

Be prepared to record events and thoughts all the time. In the car, in the doctor's office, by your bed for those three am awakenings.

Even if you record only one-twentieth of your observations, you will have plenty of grist for inspiration.

Of equal importance, especially if you don't intend to go outside your environs for speaking engagements, don't be afraid to use examples of people you know in your office, town, club, or association as inspirational vehicles.   Short of embarrassing the subject of inspiration, using stories about people that many in the group know can be very powerful because it only strengthens the closeness of the story.

Compile a phone bibliography of stories from ministers, rabbis, dentists, and other professionals. On any given day, pick up the telephone and call a minister or rabbi and ask if he would tell you his *two best* inspirational stories. To make sure he does it, explain to him what you are doing, and that you are going to speak to about a dozen ministers. Tell him that you will write down all the stories, with notes, attribute the source, and send him a copy.

Ministers keep a virtual arsenal of powerful inspirational stories at hand, and they have been tried and tested. Nevertheless, they are always running dry and will be happy to get the new material. It's a fair trade. And since only about five percent of the population goes to church on a regular basis, you don't have to worry too much about the stories being overexposed.

Dentists? Yes, because for some reason dentists, more than any other professional group I know, are loaded with inspirational stories. You may have a similar impression about some other group of professionals, doctors, or lawyers or teachers, so try them out, too.

Watch two prime-time religious programs each week. This may be difficult for many of you to do, and some of you won't be able to keep it up very long. But try it for a while because, invariably, TV evangelists and circuit preachers come up with one or two powerful inspirational stories each time they are on.

Keep in mind that these evangelists have batteries of writers whose primary job is to keep the preachers armed with inspiration.

The writers comb the world for such stories. By borrowing their stories, you can put the writers to work for you, too.

The reason you can get away with it is that the vast majority of people don't watch religious programs. Most people in your audience won't have heard the stories.

Join one or two civic clubs. Ask around among your friends to find out their opinions of the various clubs. Most clubs have guest speakers as a part of their weekly meetings. Though most are not professional-quality speakers, many will still have some good stories. Your acquaintances will have an idea of which clubs book the best speakers, and those are the ones you want to join.

Getting stories from club speakers is hit or miss. But you may get one or two good stories a month, and that is something.

A side benefit is that the club might offer you an initial speaking opportunity. Don't repeat a story to the same club from which you got it!

Go to a library one day each month. Actually, you should have been going to a library once a month, anyway, just to keep abreast of information relating to your field or for general information. Now you have a good reason. Research books and periodicals under such topics as anecdotes, illustrations, or general true-life stories or incidents.

Don't forget to look in trade and industry publications for success stories, inspiring incidents of heroism, or life-against-all-odds tales. Industry and trade publications often run such human interest stories, and you will find that these stories are often about people who are more closely related to your audiences.

The yield in inspirational stories from the library will be small, but you will leave with two or three good pieces of inspiration. That's pretty good when combined with other sources.

Purchase books of inspiration at your bookstore. I strongly urge you to buy books of philosophy, sermon illustrations, and anecdotes. Bookstores are jammed with sources that provide inspirational stories, anecdotes, and quotations.

The library of every Power Speaker should contain at least 10 books of powerful illustrations, quotes, and anecdotes. Look for books arranged topically, not alphabetically or chronologically (except for Bartlett's Book of Quotations, which everyone should have). This sort of arrangement facilitates finding the information you need.

Read a newspaper every day. A daily general-circulation newspaper is one of the best sources for inspirational stories and anecdotes; it is full of interesting tales of powerful inspiration. In fact, every day in almost every newspaper, there is at least one heartwarming story of human heroics.

Generally, if you are going to speak in another town, people you speak to will not have read the story, even if it is a news service story from AP or UPI, because city papers don't often pick up the same stories. If the story is particularly powerful or if it is about someone with whom listeners are familiar, it doesn't matter if the audience read the story, too. Tell it again.

Go to nursing homes at least twice a year and record the stories and incidents told by elderly people. Elderly people may be the best source of inspiration available, other than your own observations. You will walk away with a wealth of material, the best you can get. The stories are real. They contain life's truths, and they are from another era and have never yet been heard by later generations.

I have found it personally inspiring to just sit down with an older person and ask him to share his life experiences with me. The bonus is that I walk away with a storehouse of inspirational material that also motivates us of younger generations.

Chapter Review

- ◆ Every Power Speech uses inspiration. Inspiration is the power in Power Speaking and separates Power Speaking from ordinary public speaking.

- ◆ Constantly seek new sources of inspiration.

- ◆ Professional speakers who speak to different groups do not need to find as much inspiration as do people who speak before the same groups over and over.

- ◆ Carry a pen and pad with you at all times to record thoughts and observations on life. This is the best source for inspiration because of the genuineness and closeness to life of the stories and observations.

- ◆ Don't be afraid to use the stories of acquaintances or of people known to the group.

- ◆ Make a telephone bibliography of stories from clergy. Ask clergymen for their two best stories. Offer to give them a copy of an annotated bibliography.

- ◆ Ask dentists and other professionals about inspirational stories.

- ◆ Watch two prime-time religious shows a week. Their writers have combed the world over for good stories.

- ◆ Join one or two civic clubs that have speakers on a regular basis. Check with friends about the quality of programs at the clubs before joining.

- ◆ Spend one day each month in the library combing through books of stories, anecdotes, and illustrations. Don't forget trade and industrial journals.

- Buy books of philosophical concepts, sermon illustrations, anecdotes, and quotes. Every Power Speaker should have a library of at least 10 such books.

- Read a daily newspaper, looking for headlines that indicate human heroism kinds of stories.

- Go to nursing homes at least twice a year and let older people share their experiences. They have a wealth of inspiration with which younger generations are not familiar.

Chapter 10
How to Find and Use Humor

Finding and using humor is important to successful Power Speaking. Laughter helps relieve the tension in a presentation and, through contrast, helps keep inspiration from sounding too serious and preachy. Humor provides a springboard into illustrations and inspiration as you move the presentation toward a successful conclusion.

Even though humor is not as important an element as inspiration, you will actually need more humorous stories than inspirational illustrations because jokes become dated quickly. Here are some general rules on humor that will help in finding and using it:

Create a card file or data base to organize your jokes and anecdotes by categories. This is a good idea for both humor and inspiration. Such a catalog will be extremely important for the wealth of humor you will want to keep on file. Jokes usually have a very short life span. You have heard many jokes in your lifetime. Yet, if you were asked to tell them this very minute, you probably couldn't remember more than a few. So, try to record them when you find them.

The file or data base should be arranged by topic or key word to simplify finding the humor you need. You should also include a date on the card or in the category for each particular joke.

Only include jokes or anecdotes in your arsenal that make you laugh aloud. The acid test on humor is whether or not a joke makes you laugh; if one doesn't make you laugh aloud, forget it. Look for another.

That should be obvious, but I mention it for two reasons. First, a common notion among many speech theorists and laymen is that a moderately humorous joke is better when told to a large group. I can't imagine where the idea came from; it is false. Moderate to bad humor is moderate to bad, no matter how many people are listening. Why go for mediocrity when there is so much material available? Second, how do you expect to deliver a joke effectively when you don't even find it funny? You will become disillusioned during practice as you go over a dozen times the same joke you didn't like in the first place.

As you search for jokes, try to relate them to major ideas or themes. Chances are, by the time you start a compilation of humor, you will have an idea of some of the speeches you will construct, or the opportunities you may come upon to speak. You may not have developed major ideas or points, but you probably will have some sort of direction. Later on, as you're updating or continuing the process and already have some ideas for talks, you will have specific needs.

Pay close attention to any underlying themes or double meanings behind the joke. If you can, you might want to include a word or two on the card or in the data base relating to that theme in conjunction with the joke. This may seem to be a lot of extra work, but it will save you time later.

Remain open-minded in your approach to humor and to the individual jokes themselves. It's possible that a related idea in a joke may not strike you upon first reading, but later it will become clear. So go ahead and include in your files any good joke.

Don't use stale jokes. Usually, old jokes are stale. But this idea is a little more complex than just placing a prohibition on old humor. Often, a joke can be old even if it's been in circulation just a few weeks. So, *avoid the joke if it is one everybody is telling*.

When searching for jokes from books, a good rule to follow is that the book have a recent copyright date, preferably no more than five years old. Collections of humor in books is so often related to current issues that it is important to stay within this time frame.

Don't try impromptu humor or back-to-back jokes. Aside from the fact that two jokes back to back unbalance a point in the speech, another reason not to tell two jokes in a row is this: most speakers are not able to sustain a level of humor and command laughs continuously. In fact, about one funny joke at a time is as much as you should hope to accomplish. Many comedians don't even try it. Instead, they spend more time on the setup. They'll tell a story first, trying not to elicit too much laughter too quickly, and lead slowly, ultimately, to the finale.

As for impromptu humor, I explained why you should not succumb to the temptation to be cute or to use impromptu jokes in the introduction. Remember the belly dancers? Some speakers also believe they can be off-the-cuff after they have received some laughs during the body. Don't give in to this temptation. You don't have the time, you can't sustain the humor, and you will only digress from the speech.

Never use jokes that are in bad taste. Never tell dirty, off-color jokes, those inherently chauvinistic, racial slurs, or any jokes that could be construed as biased. You cannot put yourself in the position of offending any group or faction in the room with your humor.

Never get jokes from TV or movies. Unlike the prime-time religious shows where you might find some inspirational stories, the audiences for major sitcoms and successful movies are quite large. There is a very good chance that they will have already heard the humor from television.

Sources of Humor

Here are some examples of the best sources of humor:

Record humorous observations. Since you're already carrying around a pen and pad to record inspirational observations of life, try looking at the funnier side of life as well. This could be your best source of humor. Like inspiration, it will be better because it is real and close.

Some of the greatest humorists use this technique. They just tell the facts with a twist. Some comedians like George Carlin make a living observing the oddities of things people do. There is enough going on around you, too, that could provide a wealth of humor.

But you must record them, just as you do the inspiration, or they will evaporate. Think of the times you have awakened laughing or have caught yourself chuckling at an office mishap. Write it down! And don't forget real news stories that strike you as odd. Think how you might use them to your advantage.

Go to comedy clubs. All across the country, comedy clubs are popular. The performers are mostly up-and-coming stand-up comics with dreams of making it to the top. Their job is to keep writing and throwing out new material. Often, you will also find big-name comics at these clubs, who are trying out new material before taking it on tour. This is some of the best new material around.

So, take your pen and pad and go. It will be great fun, and you will walk away with eight to ten good new jokes that almost no one else has heard.

Buy humor and anecdote books. Go to your bookstore and find the new titles on humor and anecdotes. Remember my caution of keeping within five years on the copyright date in order to assure that your jokes are relevant to today's world.

How to Use the Humor You Find

Here are some examples of putting the humor you find to good use:

Personalize humor. I am often asked in seminars if it is permissible to lie a little bit when telling a joke. Sure, you might, but remember that all effective humor has to have some basis in reality. So, rather than lying, consider stretching the truth. Whenever you can, try to relate a joke to yourself, an aunt, a wayward brother, or perhaps some other relative. Personalizing humor always brings the joke closer to the crowd and can add a sense of tension necessary for humor to work. It will also add a touch of needed warmth.

Use visual imagery to tell a humorous story. In my speech, I could have told the joke about the fire chief this way: "And when asked what he would do with the money, the fire chief said, 'I'll probably fix the brakes on that truck.'" Instead, I said, "The ruddy-faced old fire chief wiped the sweat off his brow and spit a plug of tobacco on the ground, and said, 'Well, sir, the first thing I'm going to do is fix the brakes on that damn truck.'"

What you want to do is illustrate the story graphically so your listeners can draw a mental picture of the situation. Don't just tell them, show them. After all, the only thing they have to look at is you.

Pause until all the laughter has died down. Don't worry about not saying anything. You are in control. It is important to let the crowd quit laughing so that lingering laughter doesn't trample on the rest of your presentation.

You Can Recover From a Bomb

If you follow my instructions on how to find and use humor, you probably won't bomb. But occasionally it happens, and, more important, it worries most people.

The key to recovery is built into the very principles of Power Speaking. Your purpose is inspirational and your message is important, so bombing a joke will have minimal effect. Just say: "That's just a lighter side of this very important concept." And then continue.

Create some ideas of your own. It is easy once you realize that you won't die from a bomb. You might not need to say anything at all. Chances are, it won't happen anyway.

Chapter Review

◆ Constantly compile and update humor.

◆ Keep a card file or data base to store humor. Arrange the file topically or by key word.

◆ Never use jokes that are currently overused.

- Try to find jokes that have an underlying theme that ties into the topic.

- Speakers should only use jokes that make them laugh.

- Never use impromptu humor, follow a laugh with an attempt to be cute, or try back-to-back jokes.

- Never use off-color or offensive humor.

- The best source of humor is personal observation on life. Look on the funnier side. Record observations. Put a twist on real news stories.

- Go to comedy clubs on a regular basis as a source for the best new jokes.

- Search bookstores for new joke and anecdote books.

- The simple way to recover from a bomb is to relate it back to the speech.

Chapter 11
Preparing to Go Professional

With mastery of the Power Speaking principles comes the inclination to become a professional paid speaker on the circuit. The temptation is great because colleagues and acquaintances are constantly praising and paying tribute to you because of your remarkable speaking abilities. Some people just naturally become paid speakers. After their slow climb turns into a meteoric trip in the corporate community as a result of their enhanced communications skills, they are called on to make more and more speeches for pay. They find it beneficial and decide that going on tour may be a viable option.

The circuit's enticement is understandable. Many successful professional speakers earn $250,000 to $500,000 a year. A few earn substantially more. In addition, business opportunities which come your way on the circuit could easily double or triple that figure.

Still, there's more. Travel, for instance. It is likely that you will travel extensively, all expenses paid. It is also likely that you will be met in limos, stay in quality hotels and be taken out for expensive dinners. These are just some of the possibilities.

How many speeches do you need to make before you are ready to enter the professional speaking world? On average about 30 to 50 speeches.   Some of these may even be paid speaking engagements. But most will be free. It takes the better part of 50 speeches to develop the finesse needed to be a good speaker.

Apart from the actual practice at being a speaker, you will need certain support material to enter the speaking world. Without this material, you cannot expect to get many speaking assignments the first year, unless you have a strong personal following from past employment or professional affiliations.   Though they can be invaluable, you can not rely solely on word-of-mouth or friends your first year.

The most important materials you will need in order to get your speaking career going is a *professional-quality public relations kit* to present to those who are going to book you at banquets, corporate meetings, and conventions. Trying to book engagements the first year without such a kit is difficult. But once you have prepared your PR kit and have secured some speaking engagements, word-of-mouth will be your best advertising after the first year. Consider this when reflecting upon the importance of a PR kit: you only have one chance at a first impression.

Public Relations Kit

The public relations kit has the following key parts:

- A brochure or flyer with matching stationery
- A professionally produced audio cassette tape of a sample speech
- Endorsement letters or endorsement quotes
- A biography sheet
- A current 5" X 7" black & white photograph
- Published material including clips from articles you've written or those written about you, and any book you may have written

Brochure or Flyer

What you are trying to establish is an image, a public representation of you as a professional that is unique and striking. You want to make your brochure stand out from others. The brochure needs to be recognized, and you need name recognition. Many of the executives to whom you will send your brochures have come to expect a certain quality from the people with whom they do business. You must fulfill their expectations. Plan to spend several hundred dollars for the job; the money will be well spent.

Your brochure should probably be printed on a high quality, standard 8 1/2 X 11 format, glossy, heavy (e.g., 100 lb.) stock with at least four colors. You may want to consult a graphics artist and your printer for stock selection and color ideas for both stock and copy.

I always encourage using the services of a professional copy writer and graphics artist. Their expertise will help you devise the best copy and layout for your brochure; this is an investment that will pay off in the long run.

Here is what you should include in your brochure:

- *A powerful statement to get the attention of the reader*
- *Several of the best titles of your speeches*
- *A brief biography*
- *A bulleted list of the benefits of hiring you as a speaker*
- *Several of your best endorsements*
- *A photo of yourself*
- *Registration, cost (fee for you speech or seminar), payment (credit card, personal checks, etc.), a phone number and mail-in form for registration*

The copy you write should be simple and direct. Think about appealing to both the emotional and logical thinking of your reader. For example, an emotional appeal may include such words and phrases as "happier, boost confidence, gain respect," etc., while the logical appeal may include such ideas as "improve sales, increased earnings, become skillful," etc.

🎤 **The heading of your brochure should grab the attention and interest of the reader.** The best way to achieve this is to appeal to the reader's emotion and logic combined. For example, "Mark Yarnell's Success Seminar can increase your self confidence to dramatically increase your sales effectiveness!" or "Mark Yarnell's Power Speaking techniques dramatically enhance your personal and financial success!"

🎤 **Your speech titles should grab the attention and interest of the reader.** Meeting planners, convention planners and other interested parties want to know your topics of expertise and what your speeches are about. It is important to create a number of catchy, provocative speech titles. It may seem strange to do this when your speech will most likely be the same for each title. But that's not important. What is important is that the planners take an interest in what you have to offer. Here are some examples of several general speech titles I have used:

- A Commitment to Excellence
- Life Without Crutches
- Creating Joy in the Workplace
- Beyond Positive Thinking
- Greater Income with Enthusiasm

🎙 **Create an interesting and compelling biography of yourself to include in the brochure.** This biography should provide the highlights of your accomplishments (i.e., pertinent academic credentials, business experience, awards, etc.). This is not to be confused with the biography sheet which will be separate from your brochure, but an integral part of your PR kit.

🎙 **Endorsements of your performance as a speaker will become one of your most important sales tools.** You should include several of your most impressive endorsements or testimonials of your performance as a speaker. This should be in the form of a list similar to the endorsements on the cover of a book.

🎙 **A photo of yourself helps make a connection between you and your reader.** A clear black and white photo of yourself should be placed on the front side of your brochure. This should be a recent photo. The photo is important because it helps your reader feel a more personal connection with you once they see what you look like. The same photo may also be on your stationery and business cards.

Audio Tape

In your first year, before you are well known, meeting planners who are considering you as a speaker will most likely request a sample of your work. You can pretty much count on that nearly every time.

Never rely on a tape made at an actual presentation. The quality of tapes made at real speeches is usually very poor due to unprofessional equipment and background noises such as coughing, dinnerware clatter, etc. These days people have grown accustomed to high-quality media, and most cannot bear to listen to an unprofessional recording for more than a minute or two.

So, you should give meeting planners a quality audio tape. Most cities of any size have recording studios you can rent for a couple of hours to make your tape. You will be in a booth or room with a microphone, and the studio will provide a person to run the equipment in a control room. They will help you do the tape. You may consider dubbing in applause and laughter in appropriate places. This is an easy process and the producer can help suggest where to place audience reactions. They will have records and tapes for that, too.

For around $200 you will get a master tape, either on cassette or reel-to-reel tape. You can have cassettes copied from the master for an additional charge. If you specify the number of copies you want during the first studio session, the studio can make dozens of duplicates within minutes.

> *The length of your audio tape demo should not exceed ten minutes.*

And make sure you select your best material in a speech which you give. In fact, the first 30 seconds to a minute should immediately demonstrate that the audience loves you, that you're an excellent speaker, and that you're an expert on your subject. Meeting planners will focus on these three points in particular.

Do not attempt to submit a tape to a planner which does not apply to the topic they are interested in. In other words, if you are an expert speaker on business management don't submit a tape for a speaking engagement which focuses on motivation or sales. Stay in your area of expertise, that is, unless you have more than one area of expertise. Never try to send a tape on a topic which is unrelated and then think you can persuade the meeting planner that you can speak on just any topic. Rather, if you are an expert speaker on motivation and on sales, submit only a tape you have produced on motivation to those interested in motivation and the sales tape only to those interested in sales.

How many tapes should you make? You should probably keep between 50 to 100 tapes available to send out to bureaus and meeting planners. Also, since you will always improve your performance over time, you should update your tapes perhaps about once every year or two.

What about the packaging of the demo audio tape? It is always a good idea to present yourself in the most professional way possible. So, you may want to package your audio tape in a container which has the same color scheme and design as your stationery. You may even want to shrink-wrap your tape package just as you would for a product which you would sell.

What about video? Video is catching on very fast, but is not something which meeting planners expect of most speakers. The exception to this may be those speakers who receive in excess of $5,000 for a keynote speech 30 to 50 minutes long. But then they can afford a very nice, professionally produced video which does not exceed more than 10 minutes and which stresses the speaker's popularity with his audience, his skill as a speaker, and his expertise on his topic.

Endorsement Sheet & Letters

Endorsements or testimonials of your performance as a speaker are very important to securing speaking engagements. It is a way to demonstrate to potential buyers of your services that other people are impressed with your skills as a speaker. Endorsements can come in the form of letters or are statements of praise made by people who have attended one of your performances.

You can ask for endorsements from two sources:

> ◆ *From business colleagues and other associates who have heard you speak in your own business settings, meetings, or association gatherings. These are people who know of your speaking abilities and are willing to do you a favor.*
>
> ◆ *From listeners at early speaking engagements such as civic clubs or conventions affiliated with your industry.*

The best endorsements will of course be used in the brochure. Otherwise, you can make a comprehensive list of all your endorsements on a sheet or several sheets of paper — but try to keep it to one page, limiting your endorsements to the best ones. Also, having letters of endorsements written in your behalf are another good way to demonstrate to potential buyers of your services.

You can also get endorsements from listeners in two ways:

1. Contact the program chairman and request an endorsement.
2. As people come up to you after a speaking engagement, they will have praise or criticism; at that time, you will be in the position to ask them for endorsements.

Neither step is mutually exclusive of the other; you should do both. However, asking for a letter is self-explanatory, except that I want you to consider this: at meetings, especially civic clubs, listeners are employed by companies. Many of the listeners are important executives with those companies. When you ask them for their letters of endorsement or criticism, ask them to put it on their company letterhead.

What you may want to do to facilitate the process of getting endorsements is to prepare a letter of endorsement yourself and fax or send it to people after they have agreed to the endorsement. Offer to let them use your prepared letter or to edit it to their liking; at least they have a foundation upon which to build and are more likely to respond in a timely manner.

Biography Sheet

You will have a brief three or four sentence biography in your brochure, but you will need more than that to satisfy a meeting planner interested in hiring you as a speaker. So, you are going to make an expanded biography which includes a detailed list of your accomplishments. This will be your biography sheet, which is literally one or two pages long and will become an important part of your public relations kit. Now, you may want to start with this first because thinking of what might be relevant accomplishments is usually the hardest part of writing the copy.

A trick to help overcome that block is to have a friend with you when you are thinking about it. Try telling your friend about what you have done in the past. Invariably, they will ask questions about details that you had submerged in your memory. Often, those details, or gaps, turn out to be relevant and valuable experiences. After a few minutes, you have an impressive list of accomplishments.

Try to focus on functions and the people affected by the things you have done. Also, boast of your latest book, recent articles you've written (particularly if you're published in widely known magazines such as Time, or McCall's, etc.), national TV appearances (e.g., Oprah, Donahue, etc.), and other interesting and notable points which distinguish you from other speakers in the same field. But keep this brief and simple.

When you are going through this exercise, keep this in the back of your mind: everybody's life experiences are valuable if they have learned from them and can communicate what they have learned. Most people in the world cannot communicate that knowledge well. That is why there are so many audiences and listeners and very few speakers.

Current Black & White Photo

Make it a current photo. You would be surprised how many so-called professional speakers use photos in their PR material that are many years removed from their real age. A good 5" X 7" glossy black and white photo is sufficient for your public relations kit. This photo may be the same photo used in your brochure. Color is not necessary, since black and white is easier to reproduce should a meeting planner decide to use your photo in promotional material.

Published Material

In your effort to secure speaking engagements, the more famous you are, the more in demand you become, and the more money you can demand for your services.

One quick way to become famous is to be published. If you have published a book in your area of expertise, by all means, include a copy of your book with your public relations material. This is very impressive to meeting planners. If you have not published a book, you should make every attempt to be published in magazines and trade journals in your field. This not only enhances your credibility as an expert in your field, but also makes you more famous and known in the field — a fact which can directly lead to well paid speaking engagements.

Even if you aren't a particularly good writer, develop a good idea for an article. You can always find good editing help after you have written down your ideas.

There are two ways to go about it. Since your main purpose is not to be a professional writer, go ahead and write the article, get editing help and submit the article to a local business magazine. You might get published because you're a professional in your field writing about a subject of interest to the readership. The editors will recognize that and perhaps publish your article.

However, if you want to get quite a few articles published, first call to discuss a possible article idea with those magazines most likely to publish your type of article. Then, learn to write a good query letter. The *Writer's Market*, an annual publication listing book publishers and magazines, is an excellent place to start when looking for potential magazines in which to publish.

What is a query letter? A query letter is a short letter, usually one page or less, which states your article idea, your background, and why a publication's readership would be interested in reading the article. Most major publications give assignments on query letters only, and smaller publications are starting to do the same thing. Most beginning writers try to avoid queries because they believe it is as much trouble to write the letter as it is the article; this is a false assumption. The query letter is a valuable sales tool in publishing.

People tend to accord an unusual amount of respect to authors in the business community. If you address an issue of importance to those in the business community, you gain instant status that puts you a notch above other speakers. It isn't unusual to be asked to speak solely on the merits of what you have written.

Additional useful published materials are clips of articles written either about you directly or about a book or books you have written, or possibly even articles about a speech you gave at some special function. Keep track of publications which feature you and your accomplishments and collect the articles. Make copies of these articles and include them as part of your public relations kit. Obviously, any published material about you can only enhance your image.

Chapter Review

- A professional-quality public relations kit is essential to booking engagements during your first year as a professional.

- After the first year, word-of-mouth advertising should be enough for Power Speakers.

- The PR kit will have the following parts: a brochure and matching stationery; an audio tape of a sample speech; endorsement letters and endorsement quotes; a biography sheet; a recent black & white photo; and any published material you have published or has been published about you.

- Hire a professional graphic designer to create a logo and to do all brochure, packaging design and layout work.

- Telling accomplishments to a friend will help you remember details of past accomplishments and determine which accomplishments are important.

- Use a current black and white photo made by a professional.

- Endorsements come from two sources:
  1. From colleagues and associates
  2. From listeners at early engagements such as civic clubs

- Use excerpts from the best endorsements for the brochure.

- Get endorsements from listeners two ways:
  1. Contact the program chairman and request an endorsement.
  2. As people come up to you after an early speaking engagement, they will have praise or criticism; at that time, you will be in the position to ask them for endorsements.

◆ Draft 20 catchy speech titles. They should be general and are designed to stimulate the interest of the program chairman.

◆ Hire a writer to write and proof the copy both before and after layout.

◆ Print the brochure on a single 8 1/2 by 11 sheet of heavy paper.

◆ Record a sample speech on audio tape at a professional recording studio.   Never use a tape made at an actual presentation as conditions are not usually conducive for a professional-quality tape.

◆ The tape is necessary because in the first months of your speaking career, decision makers will want a sample.

Chapter 12
How to Obtain Speaking Engagements

Now that you have public relations materials, you're faced with the challenge of how to book speaking engagements. Keep this in mind: *there are no definite rules.* However, I can offer the following suggestions that are proven to be invaluable in launching your professional speaking career.

Speakers Bureaus

There are essentially two ways to market yourself in an effort to secure speaking engagements. You can book *yourself* for speaking engagements or you can use the services of speakers bureaus or booking agencies, as they are sometimes called. Generally, most speakers combine their own efforts with the efforts of several speakers bureaus — which is what I recommend. I'll explain here briefly about speakers bureaus and how they work for you.

A speakers bureau is a company which specializes in matching speaking engagements with speakers who they have carefully screened to be part of their bureau. If you project a professional image and have a good public relations kit, you can most likely find a speakers bureau willing to represent you to their clients. There are several hundred speakers bureaus in North America. Speakers bureaus are generally divided into two broad types: those who book speakers able to demand in excess of $5,000 per engagement, and those who demand less than $5,000 per engagement. As a general rule, all speakers bureaus will take up to 35% of the speaker's fee to book a speaker. This may sound like a big chunk, but speakers bureaus definitely work for their money. Keep in mind that to make you worth their effort, you must charge at least $500 or more as a speaker.

> *Currently, $500 per engagement is the minimum fee for the average professional speaker.*

Usually, speakers bureaus have a number of regular clients with whom they work, and take care of everything including phone calls, faxes, mailing of PR kits, negotiating speaking agreements, and everything else. The business of speakers bureaus is very time, money, and work intensive, so a favorable rapport with a good speakers bureau can help a speaker make a very good living.

The most effective way to get a speakers bureau to work for you is to make personal contact with the people running the bureau. But don't wait for them to call; take the initiative and maintain ongoing contact to see how prospects are developing. One good speakers bureau is equivalent to knowing dozens of meeting planners who may be interested in your services. The time and effort you spend to develop a favorable rapport with a speakers bureau (and you will want several of them working for you) will be highly beneficial.

How do you find speakers bureaus? The Yellow Pages list speakers bureaus under speakers bureaus, booking agencies or lecture bureaus. Send them your PR kit and follow up with a phone call.

Marketing Yourself

Like any other business, the speaking business requires an ongoing marketing effort. The nice thing is, the first year is the most challenging, after which you will have gained recognition and the bookings come more easily. At that point you can also charge higher fees.

Who hires speakers and who can you contact in an attempt to secure speaking engagements? Here is a list of the most likely organizations to hire you as a speaker:

- **Businesses** of all sorts, but particularly businesses which are sales oriented such as car dealerships, multi-level marketing companies, insurance agencies, realtors, etc.
- **Business and trade associations** — they always have annual or biannual conferences or conventions, and some even have monthly meetings which feature speakers.
- **Church groups** of all sorts; these hire a variety of speakers, often self-help, motivational, inspirational, etc.
- **Civic groups**, such as the Kiwanis club, the Lions club, the local Chamber of Commerce, etc.
- **Convention or meeting planners** who book trade shows and various conferences, usually business oriented.
- **Fraternal organizations** — if you are a member of college fraternity or some other fraternal organization, contact them.
- **Professional organizations** which of course means doctors, lawyers, dentists, engineers, etc. Some speakers not only speak to these groups on general topics, but also offer seminars for large amounts of money to instruct these professionals on some aspect of their profession to enhance their skills or practices.

Civic Groups

During the initial months as a professional speaker, your first goal is to get as much exposure as possible. I have received innumerable paid speaking opportunities from people who heard me at Lions and Rotary clubs. The clubs have a diverse membership, many of whom are key people in corporations or associations who are giving something back to the community. They appreciate your presence and contribution to the club and enjoy listening to you. You get to advertise in an environment close to their hearts. In addition, another benefit of speaking free to clubs is that it's a good place to get first endorsements, for instance from these key executives, upon which you will rely for future contacts. You can obtain a list of all clubs and organizations from any local Chamber of Commerce.

You won't have to give free speeches very long, but the ones you do give will help immensely. Everyone in business has to give out free samples once in a while.

Mailing Lists

One effective way to reach your potential clients is to get a mailing list. Then mail out your brochure to about 20 prospects at a time per month. Mail to a specific person if possible, and follow up each mailing with a phone call. Never do such a mailing without a phone call. You still may run into problems getting the person you want, but you will get through more easily if the person has seen a brochure.

While you patiently phone and phone again to catch the person in the office, never be rude or abrasive with secretaries or assistants. These people are a direct link to your first impression with CEOs, etc. Often, they make the decisions on speakers for meetings because the boss doesn't want to take the time to bother with it, or is uncertain about what to do.

How do you get mailing lists? You can begin by checking your Yellow Pages to find a particular group, business or organization. Sales-related companies are usually plentiful in most medium or large cities. These type of companies are excellent opportunities for a speaker to wield his craft. The best sales companies to pursue are insurance companies, manufacturers of products for retail outlets such as candy and food companies, clothing manufacturers and distributors, high-tech companies, and any other group that depends on a large sales force. Sales-oriented companies hold at least one major meeting a year, sometimes 10 to 15. These meetings often require paid speakers. So, send a package to the company and then follow up with a phone call.

Most libraries have directories which list the group, business or organization you wish to contact. Ask the librarian for some assistance. Tell them you want names of key people, mailing addresses, and phone numbers if possible. Another possibility is to rent very specific mailing lists through your local mailing list broker. Again, be very clear what you want and have the broker work for you to get the list you want.

Association Membership

You should become a member of the association in your field of expertise. And you should also join your state's association of association executives.

One example of these associations is the American Society of Association Executives, which has affiliates in every state in the country. The membership is composed of key executives from every major association in that state. From the AMA to the Cattle Breeders Association, these associations represent millions of people and all major industries.

> *Professional associations pay some of the highest fees in America for both consultants and circuit banquet speakers.*

As a member, you will be exposed to all these contacts and will also get an idea of their needs. The fee to join is only $100 to $200. The good news is that most speakers do not make the effort to join these organizations. Make sure you go to the meetings, and take a few brochures. You will be rewarded.

Toastmasters Membership

Toastmasters provides a good forum for practice once you know Power Speaking principles. Also, in putting the principles to good use, your proficiency and abilities will attract other members to you, and you may become an officer in the local organization. If you become president or a major officer in a local chapter of Toastmasters, your name goes on a mailing list that goes to many of the largest corporations in America. Often, companies assume that if you are a Toastmasters officer, then you must be a good speaker. So, frequently these corporations will ask you to speak at their functions.

Referrals

You will most likely get referrals and the number of referrals will increase the more you perform. If you are good at what you do, people will appreciate this and will gladly refer you to other groups in the same organization or field, or perhaps provide endorsements to help you get bookings in related fields. I have known of speakers who began speaking before one group, say bankers, and before long branched out to speak before groups of financial planners, real estate people, etc., all because of the referrals they received from the banking community. One opportunity often leads to another. You should see referrals go into effect after your first year as a professional speaker.

Newsletters

Newsletters are a good way to promote yourself to people who have attended your speeches. At the conclusion of your speeches you can have a card that everyone fills out, providing their names and addresses. This becomes your mailing list. The newsletters can be a simple one page quarterly publication which features two or three interesting articles or excerpts from a book or books you've written. You can also feature reviews of your own work or the works of others you recommend and possibly sell through your newsletter. Most importantly, list the cities and places where you are scheduled to speak and invite your readers to contact your office should they wish to book you for a speaking engagement. The newsletter can be a very effective marketing tool. And the cost to produce a newsletter for a full year can be easily paid for with one speaking engagement you have booked as a result of its distribution.

Selling Your Services at Hotels

Now here is a marketing idea that may not suit everyone, but can be very effective for those who are bold enough and eager enough to give their speaking careers this kind of jumpstart. I have used this method and it really got my career going.

As many of you know, it is often impossible to reach key executives on the telephone, unless you are already a key executive of another firm with whom they do business. Even then it can be difficult. My hotel approach is designed to counter this problem.

Anywhere from five to ten meetings are held at each major hotel in major cities every working day of the year. At every one of those meetings are program chairmen or CEOs, or at least someone in leadership.

What you need to do is pick a quality hotel, take brochures and business cards, and spend a morning meeting salesmen, managers, corporate leaders, and program directors.

Wait until a meeting takes a break. As people leave the meeting room, stop any individual and find out the name of the program coordinator. Once you find the right person, simply walk up and introduce yourself. Explain that you don't want to take much time, you know how busy he is, but you wanted to stop by and bring him a brochure, talk for just a minute, and perhaps give him a sample tape. Explain that in the future, you would very much like to address his group.

Any good salesperson knows that unless you can get to the person who can say "yes," you're wasting your time. The problem is, it's difficult to get to that person. In hotels, you can. You catch CEOs or program directors off guard; their defenses are down, and they are impressed with your initiative. You are not just a piece of paper or a voice on a tape. You are a viable candidate standing before them.

You could even get lucky and book an engagement on the spot. Once, in Austin, Texas, I approached a business leader at a medical association meeting. After suggesting that I would like to speak to the group in the future, this leader invited me in to speak then and there, and paid me $500 on the spot. As it turned out, they desperately needed a banquet speaker because the scheduled speaker was sick and couldn't make it.

You never know what can happen until you try. But think of this: if you are extremely industrious, in one morning you can go to three major hotels and hand out 20 to 30 brochures. You place your brochures in the hands of the leading people from all kinds of organizations, industries, associations, and trades.

Speaking Fees

I mentioned that often the only difference between being a professional speaker and an amateur is that the professional gets paid. But how do you negotiate for that pay?

Unfortunately, many meeting planners have gotten off cheap. They let people assume they don't have much money to spend, or they get away with not paying a speaker because they assume, or the speaker assumes, they are doing a speaker a favor by letting him speak. Nothing is further from the truth.

Most groups and corporations have thousands of dollars budgeted for speakers' fees. Of course, they are going to pay as little as they can. There are ways to get fees up without looking greedy.

Negotiating Speaking Fees

When talking with a meeting planner, program director or other executive in charge of booking, simply ask how much their organization has budgeted for speakers. Generally, they will indicate a range for what they want to spend.

However, in some rare cases they won't commit to any numbers. All you have to say, then, is that your fee is $1,000 to $5,000. If they say $500 is all they ever spend, then you have a choice to make.

If you don't want to speak for $500, either say no, or maintain your fee position and hope they counteroffer with a more acceptable price. If, however, you really would be happy to speak for $500, the way around your initial fee statement is to say, "How long would the speech last?" When they respond with a time of 20 minutes, you might reply that you thought they were talking about a half-day seminar and that you would be happy to come speak to their group for $500.

Make your own rules. If you are willing to negotiate, you will be successful. I know of no other area of business in America today, except perhaps for writing and the movies, where you can openly argue and negotiate so easily with the president of a major corporation.

Do keep this in the back of your mind when you go to negotiate: if the group wants you badly enough, if you have presented yourself well, then they will alter the meeting budget to pay your price.

How do you decide what to charge as a speaking fee? To begin with, you should probably start at no less than $500 per speaking engagement; this is about the average for a beginning professional speaker. Then, when you are discussing a possible speaking engagement with a meeting planner, you must find out several things before you set your price. First, find out the amount of money they have allocated for speakers. Most will give you a number. If they say $5,000 and you have never made more than $500 for a speech, simply say, "that will be acceptable."

Here are the most important variables in establishing fees:

- What is the topic of the speech?
- How long should the speech be: 20 minutes, 1 hour, 1/2 day, a full day seminar?
- How many people do you expect to attend this event?
- Will you publicize this event, and if so, in what way?
- Who was the last speaker for this event?

If you have been paid $500 in the past for a 20 minute speech, and they want you to conduct a 1/2 day seminar before several hundred people, for an event which will receive TV and newspaper publicity, you may want to charge $1,500 or $2,000. All this, of course, is negotiable. Another variable that comes into the picture is the location of the event. Is it within driving distance, or will it require air travel to get to the event? If so, the fee must be increased. Normally, the fee is separate from travel expenses, hotel accommodations, meal expenses, cab fair, etc. Always charge your speaking fee plus expenses.

As you become more famous and in demand, you will eventually have to increase your fees. Many professional speakers increase their fees annually. You know you must increase your fee when you look at your calendar for the next six months and you are almost completely booked. The old supply and demand axiom applies: since you're more in demand, you can demand more in fees.

What about speakers bureaus? To keep things simple, it is always better to let a speakers bureau negotiate the fee for you if they were the ones to make the initial contact with a potential client. They have been in the business long enough to know what you're worth. Also it is a good idea to let them have their commission for a speaking engagement they have booked even if the meeting planner came to you first. This especially applies to circumstances when you give a speech booked by a bureau and afterwards you are given an opportunity to speak through a meeting planner who may have been in the audience to see your performance. Rather than dealing directly with the meeting planner, inform them that you wish to go through the bureau who had booked you for the event where they saw you.

Ultimately, it is always to your advantage to let bureaus negotiate your fees and to let them get their commission. Why? Because it builds trust between you and the bureau and you will be on the top of their list when new speaking opportunities for which you are qualified come along. In short, it pays in the end to deal honestly and generously with speaker bureaus.

Booking

Booking is a speakers industry term used to describe being scheduled for a speaking engagement. As you will initially be doing much of your own marketing, you will probably book most of your speaking engagements (as much as 80 percent), even though you have several speakers bureaus promoting you. Before the actual booking, of course, you will most likely have sent the meeting planner your PR kit and they may even have attended one of your speeches to evaluate your performance. You then find out all about the event, the date of the event, its location, and negotiate the fee plus expenses.

Once a price has been agreed upon, you must secure the deal with a written agreement. Some speakers use letters which spell out their terms, but most speakers use contracts. A contract should indicate who the speaker is and with whom he is contracted. The contract will also include the location, date, specific time when the speaker is expected to attend the event for the speech, duration of the speech, the name or topic of the event, and the specification that the company retaining you is responsible for all expenses. The fee should be made clear and an advance deposit of 25 to 50 percent of the fee should be made upon signing the agreement.

An agreement contract is more formal and more professional than a letter. This adds to your image and makes it less likely that anything will be overlooked when closing the deal. For examples of agreements, you can consult your local Toastmasters, contact the National Speakers Association (address in Sources section), or consult the books I recommend at the end of this book.

Much of what I have suggested in the last two chapters takes considerable time, effort, and money. But think of the rewards. Many of us who want to speak on a full or part time professional basis will only use a few of these suggestions. I highly recommend you try as many as possible. You will become a major speaker on the circuit a lot quicker if you do.

> *In the long run, the best advertisement for a Power Speaker is word of mouth.*

The suggestions in these chapters are only to get people talking about you in the first place. After about a year, your emphasis won't be placed as heavily on these promotional techniques. Instead, you'll be like many others who have applied Power Speaking principles. You'll have to say no 10 or 20 times a month, and you will worry more about burnout and how to invest your money than obtaining more engagements.

Chapter Review

- There are no rules in booking speaking engagements.

- Get mailing lists of businesses, associations, and civic clubs from local chambers of commerce. However, never do a bulk mailing.

- Make selected mailings of about 20 brochures a month and always follow up with phone calls.

- Establish a good rapport with secretaries and assistants. Often they are the people who really decide on the speaker.

- Find sales-related companies — manufacturers, food processors, large insurance companies — any firm with a large sales force. Use the Yellow Pages.

- Sales-related companies have one major event a year, often many more and usually they have paid speakers.

- Join state associations of association executives in order to meet key people representing all major industries in the state. Associations pay some of the highest fees in the nation for speaking and consulting.

- Become a member of a local Toastmasters club. Toastmasters is a good practice forum. The names of people who become officers are placed on mailing lists that go to major industries; companies throughout the nation often book speakers from the list.

- Make free speeches to civic clubs, organizations, and associations your first year. Their diverse memberships include executives from companies that will hire speakers after hearing a free sample.

- Join local speakers bureaus to keep updated on events in town and to help with bookings.

- Go to major hotels in major cities to meet the people responsible for booking engagements. They are easier to meet at hotel events and are usually more receptive. The advantage is meeting and placing materials into the hands of the people who can say "yes."

- When negotiating a speaking fee, ask the decision maker his parameters. If they don't give any numbers, give a range such as $1,000 to $5,000.

- If they counter and say they only pay $500, either hold to your price and hope they come up or say "no," if you are unwilling to speak for their price. If you are willing to speak for the smaller amount, then go ahead.

- Remember that budgets can be changed or rearranged if an organization really wants a speaker badly enough.

Chapter 13
The Scope of Power Speaking

It is to your advantage to think of all the different ways and circumstances to use Power Speaking. I developed Power Speaking as a successful method to get standing ovations with formal speeches in very formal settings. For what I had anticipated, it worked great! But, as with any new system, I couldn't envision all the uses and benefits of Power Speaking until I had worked with it a while, because I could only rely on the result of old systems.

What happened with Power Speaking was this: the principles worked great in the formal settings for which they were originally designed. In fact, they worked so well that I was often swept from the stage with congratulations and requests for my opinions and insight on every imaginable topic. I was even asked to consult various business leaders for help in other ventures.

As time went on, more and more people asked me to teach them Power Speaking. As more and more people started using the techniques, I found they were using it in a variety of settings and circumstances, and they were reporting back to me the remarkable results. These Power Speakers were becoming powers in every facet of their lives. Incomes soared, job opportunities and advancement abounded. As people overcame one major fear, other fears vanished as well. It is easy to understand: people who had received very little recognition were suddenly awash in accolades.

How did this happen? It happened simply because these people found a way to communicate messages in the marketplace with power and inspiration, a skill that, until now, has waned into near extinction in corporate America.   These users of Power Speaking principles created a niche for themselves, a new market, and filled it with good communication.

To fully apply the principles, what I and these other Power Speakers had to do was to see possibilities and apply the principles.

> *There are almost limitless applications and I've observed over the years that the more people use Power Speaking principles, the more influential they become.*

These are just a few examples of the broad adaptability of Power Speaking. I have also shown you the benefits that have come to specific individuals who have seen the possibilities through the adaptability of Power Speaking and who have chosen not to lock themselves into limitations and past knowledge. They have moved and motivated themselves to become recognized powers by overcoming fear and by using the resources they had available.

I know that speaking in public is not life itself. But to many people who have learned this simple way of improving their positions in life, they have unlocked other secrets to powerful living, an awakening once the first light was let in.

I urge you to use the principles in good faith. Believe that there can be simple means to receive tremendous benefits. Write and let me know how it is going. You could be my newest and most powerful inspirational story!

Sources

These sources were very helpful in writing this book and can be valuable in your effort to succeed as a Power Speaker.

Books to Help Your Speaking

3500 Good Quotes for Speakers, Gerald F. Lieberman (Doubleday, 1993)

And I Quote: The Definitive Collection of Quotes, Sayings, and Jokes for the Contemporary Speechmaker, Ashton Applewhite, ed. (St. Martin's Press, 1992)

Bartlett's Familiar Quotations, John Bartlett (Little, Brown, 1992)

The Beacon Book of Quotations By Women, Rosalie Maggio, ed. (Beacon Press, 1992)

The Fourth and By Far the Most Recent 637 Best Things Anybody Ever Said, Robert Byrne (Fawcett Books, 1990)

The Great Thoughts, George Seldes, ed. (Ballantine, 1990)
   A collection of wisdoms and quotes from the Abelard to Zola, from ancient Greece to contemporay America of the ideas that have shaped the history of the world.

How To Make A Fortune From Public Speaking, Dr. Robert Anthony (Berkley Books, 1985)
   This covers the basics of getting started as a professional speaker. Read this book first, and then read Dottie Walter's book, *Speak and Grow Rich*.

More Podium Humor, James C. Humes (Harper-Collins, 1993)

New York Public Library Book of 20th Century American Quotations, Stephen Donadio, ed. (Warner Books, 1992)
The Oxford Dictionary of Quotations, 4th ed. (Oxford University Press, 1992)

Podium Humor, James C. Humes (Harper-Collins, 1985)

The Power of Positive Living, Norman Vincent Peale (Fawcett Crest, 1990)
   The late Mr. Peale was a personal friend of mine, and has written many books which can serve as excellent sources for true inspirational stories. He is one of the early positive thinking gurus.

Power Quotes, Daniel B. Baker (Visible Ink Press, 1992)

Speak And Grow Rich, Dottie Walters & Lilly Walters (Prentice Hall, 1989)
   This is an excellent book about how to enter the professional speaking world the fastest and best way. Dottie Walters is one of the premier speakers and speakers bureau professionals.

Speaker's Library of Business Stories, Anecdotes and Humor, Joe Griffith (Prentice Hall, 1990)

Speaker's Sourcebook II, Quotes, Stories & Anecdotes for Every Occasion, Glen Van Ekeren (Prentice Hall, 1994)

Words of Wisdom, William Safire and Leonard Safir, eds. (Simon and Schuster, 1990)

Books to Help You Book Engagements

ASAE Directory, c/o of American Society of Association Executives, 1575 Eye St., N.W. Washington D.C. 20005
     Write to this address for this list of speakers, speaking sites (i.e., conventions), and services for those who arrange association events.

Corporate Meeting Planners Directory, 1140 Broadway New York, NY 10001
     Write to this address for this directory.

Direct Mail Lists Rates and Data, 5201 Old Orchard Rd., Skokie IL 60067
     Write to this address for this book as it is an excellent source for mailing lists.

Encyclopedia of Associations, Book Tower Detroit MI 48226
     This lists all the major associations in America. A good source for getting names, addresses and information about American associations. Check your library for this publication.

Meeting and Event Planning Guide, 2811 Wilshire Blvd., Suite 430 Santa Monica, CA 90403
     Write to this address for this directory.

Meeting News Directory, 1515 Broadway New York, NY 10036
     Write to this address for this directory.

Nationwide Directory of Association Meeting Planners, 1140 Broadway New York NY 10001

Write to this address for this directory or it may be available in a well-stocked library. It is an excellent source listing association meeting planners, the people you need to get acquainted with to make bookings.

Nationwide Directory of Corporate Meeting Planners, 1140 Broadway New York NY 10001

This is another important directory which may be available in a well-stocked library. This is an excellent source which lists meeting planners of the largest corporations in America, the people you need to get acquainted with to make bookings.

The Newsletter Handbook, Wesley Dorsheimer (Hippocrene Books, 1993)

World Convention Dates, 79 Washington Street, Hempstead NY 11550

Write to these people to subscribe to this very useful publication.

Books to Help You Get Published

Beginner's Guide to Getting Published (Writer's Digest Books, 1994)

The Chicago Manual of Style, 14th ed. (University of Chicago Press, 1993)

Get Published, Diane Gage and Marcia Coppess (Henry Holt & Co., 1994)

A good reference for getting published in magazines.

Handbook of Magazine Article Writing, Jean M. Fredette, ed. (Writer's Digest Books, 1988)

How to Get Happily Published, 4th ed., Judith Applebaum (Harper Collins, 1992)

International Directory of Little Magazines and Small Presses (Dustbooks)
    This is a good source for a comprehensive list of trade publications for your writing efforts. Consult a copy at your library.

The Writer's Digest Guide to Manuscript Formats, Dian Buchman (Writer's Digest Books, 1987)

Writer's Market, Mark Garvey, ed. (Writer's Digest Books)
    This is a directory of book publishers and magazines useful for finding markets for your articles. Updated annually and available in most bookstores.

Writing with Power, Peter Elbou (Oxford University Press, 1981)

Organizations

    Here are the names and addresses of several organizations you should either join or learn more about.

American Society of Association Executives
1575 Eye St., NW
Washington DC 20005-1168

International Platform Association
2564 Berkshire Rd.
Cleveland Heights OH 44106

National Speakers Association
3877 N. 7th Street, Suite 350
Phoenix AZ 85014

Toastmasters International
2200 North Grand Avenue
Santa Ana CA 92711

Professional Speakers Association
3540 Wilshire Blvd., Suite 310
Los Angeles CA 90010

Companies for Professional Speakers

Here are some companies which may be useful in helping you with your career as a professional speaker:

Copley Photo Service
Box 190
San Diego CA 92112
A low cost, high quality black and white photo duplicating service.

Fleetwood Company
Boston, MA
(800) 458-8273
A good company for audio tape duplication.

Kessler Management
10747 Wilshire Blvd., Suite 807
Los Angeles CA 90024
This company is known for speaker management and public relations.

Newsletter Clearinghouse
44 W. Market St.
PO Box 311
Rhinebeck NY 15272
This company can help you produce newsletters.

Paper Chase Press
5721 Magazine St., Suite 152
New Orleans LA 70115
Book publishing and publicity. Some subsidy publishing.

Southwest Cassettes
3470 E. Paradise Dr.
Phoenix AZ 85028
Another good company for audio tape duplication.

INDEX

About the Author

Mark Yarnell has been a professional speaker for nearly twenty years and is known for his speeches and seminars on professional speaking, motivation and multi-level marketing. As contributing editor to *Success* magazine, Mark Yarnell has written many articles on each of these topics.

Mark has also distinguished himself by receiving the American Dream Award from the Howard Ruff company for parlaying $179 of borrowed capital into an International Network that created numerous millionaires and achieves over $70 million in annual sales.

Formerly a minister, Mark enjoys his role as a philanthropist. He is a member of the De Tocqueville Society, having donated the largest single gift in the history of Nevada to the United Way in Reno. He established and personally funds the only free treatment program in Nevada for alcoholics and addicts, School of Sobriety, now endorsed by many area judges.

Mark lives with his wife, Rene, and their two children in Reno, Nevada.

- NOTES -

- NOTES -

Books, Tapes, & Articles

Mark Yarnell and his wife Rene have authored several books and numerous articles on speaking, networking and multi-level marketing. They have also produced tapes on these topics. For ordering or information on any of these products call:

800/458-8273 (TAPE)

Power Speaking Audio Tape

The audio version of this book, *Power Speaking*, is available by ordering either by phone, by filling out and sending the order form below, or through select major bookstores. For phone orders call: 800/458-8273.

Order Form

Please send me _____ copy(ies) of *Power Speaking* trade paperback @ $14.95 each.

Please send me _____ audio tape(s) of *Power Speaking* one 90 minute tape @ $14.95 each.

NAME:_____

ADDRESS:_____

Fill out form and send check or money order in U.S. funds. All payments made to: PAPER CHASE PRESS
Send orders to:
PAPER CHASE PRESS
5721 Magazine St., Suite 152, New Orleans LA 70115
Add $2.00 shipping & handling for each book or audio tape ordered in the U.S. ($4.00 for S&H outside U.S.). For orders in Louisiana, add 9% sales tax. Allow 4 to 6 weeks for delivery.

One WaCKY FaMiLY

Illustrated by Disney Global Artists

A Random House PICTUREBACK® Book
Random House 🏠 New York

Copyright © 2004 Disney Enterprises, Inc. All rights reserved under International and Pan-American Copyright Conventions.
Published in the United States by Random House Children's Books, a division of Random House, Inc., New York, NY 10019,
and simultaneously in Canada by Random House of Canada Limited, Toronto, in conjunction with Disney Enterprises, Inc.
PICTUREBACK, RANDOM HOUSE, and the Random House colophon are registered trademarks of Random House, Inc.
Library of Congress Control Number: 2003103336
ISBN: 0-7364-2211-0
www.randomhouse.com/kids/disney
Printed in the United States of America   10 9 8 7 6 5 4 3 2

© Disney

When Stitch, Jumba, and Pleakley arrived in Hawaii, they became part of Lilo's family. Now this crazy group is about to get even crazier!

Stitch has 625 cousins, and they've all landed on Earth. They are genetic experiments, just like Stitch, and they all have their own special skills. Just wait until you meet them. . . .

Cannonball

Roly-poly Experiment 520 makes a giant splash wherever it goes. Cannonball creates waves so humongous, they can cover the Hawaiian Islands in a blanket of water!

Experiment 501 likes to squirt water.

Yin

© Disney

Yang

Experiment 502 is hot stuff—it spouts lava!
Separately these two experiments are dangerous,
but put Yin and Yang together, and they have the
capability to create a whole new island!

Mr. Stenchy

Awww! Experiment 254 is so adorable! Don't you want to take it home with you? Bad idea—once there, Mr. Stenchy turns into a not-so-cute stink bomb!

© Disney

When Experiment 513 walks by, you'll know it! Richter makes supersized earthquakes with his superstrong tail.

Sprout

Be careful what you feed Experiment 509! Sprout may look like a harmless plant, but when it gobbles down Jumba's megafertilizer, it grows into a mean, massive forest—with an appetite for destruction!

Experiment 601 is a kickboxing machine.
If you need something kicked, call on Kixx!

Gigi

© Disney

You may not believe that Experiment 007 was created in outer space—it looks like a little dog. But once Gigi opens its mouth, you'll want to send it to the moon! It will drive you crazy with its nonstop yapping.

Fibber

Experiment 032 is a living, breathing lie detector. Fibber buzzes whenever it hears a fib. So be good and tell the truth!

Phantasmo

© Disney

Boo! Ghostly Experiment 375 can bring any object to life. If your pencils start dancing on the table, Phantasmo is probably to blame!

Love is in the air when Experiment 323 is around. With a peck of its tiny beak, Hunkahunka makes you fall in love with the next person you see!

© Disney

Hunkahunka

Lilo did a good job helping Stitch learn how to behave himself. Hopefully she can do the same for the wacky new members of the family!

© Disney